PALM COURT

ROBERT OVERTON

Palm Court

Illustrations by John Lawrence

Hamish Hamilton . London

First published in Great Britain 1979
by Hamish Hamilton Ltd
Garden House 57-59 Long Acre London WC2E 9JZ

Published in the United States of America
by Hamish Hamilton Ltd in association with
David & Charles Inc, North Pomfret, Vermont 05053, USA

British Library Cataloguing in Publication Data

Overton, Robert
    Palm court.
    1.   Courts — Persian Gulf States — Anecdotes,
    facetiae, satire, etc.   2.   Courts — Islands
    of the Pacific — Anecdotes, facetiae, satire
    etc.
    I.   Title
    347′ .536′010924   [Law]   79-40459
    ISBN 0-241-10110-7

Filmset by Pioneer
Printed and bound in Great Britain by
Redwood Burn Ltd, Trowbridge and Esher

CONTENTS

Chapter One

Confessions of a Judge

Towards the end of 1882, after a diplomatic reception at Windsor Castle, there was found left behind in the Music Room a curiously shaped parcel. 'For personal delivery into the hands of Her Majesty', read the label. The wrappings were opened, somewhat gingerly, by a gentleman usher over a bucket of water, for the Queen's life had recently been threatened in anarchist quarters.

To everyone's surprise the parcel contained the war club of a fellow Queen, Fatu Hova IV of the Savage Isles, which lie between Fiji and New Guinea. It was inlaid with a pattern of ivory, which on closer inspection turned out to be human teeth formed into a kind of grimace. It was accompanied by a simple message, translated into English copperplate:

'In ceding her South Pacific territory to Victoria, Queen Fatu Hova IV abandons the law of the club and all cannibal customs in exchange for the Laws of England. With this emblem of the past the Queen sends a big smile for Victoria, fully entrusting her and her successors to govern the Savage Isles in accordance with British Honour and Justice.'

The offering had been made by Queen Fatu to Captain Montagu, RN, when he incorporated the Savage Islands into the British Empire upon the Flag-Raising Expedition of March 1882. Once the package came under Victoria's inspection, Her Imperial Majesty was appropriately moved by the wording of the message, if somewhat startled by the gift itself.

Club law exchanged for the Laws of England. A debatable swop for any respectable Savage Islander whose prestige depended on eating his enemies dispatched by the club. It was part of the bargain, of course, that Whitehall would send a judge to the South Seas and I am the last of the line.

1

Much the same thing went on throughout the Victorian Empire. Neither Victoria nor her Imperial advisers doubted the civilising effect that English Law would have upon the grateful natives. Later it became fashionable to speak of English Law abroad as 'an alien code that had nothing to do with the natural rhythm of the lives of indigenous peoples'.

All I can say is from my point of view our law proved extremely serviceable. The travelling set of Halsburys *Laws of England* is no featherweight companion. Its forty-two volumes fill the Kitchener Safari Trunk (Model 3). This formidable compendium saw me through a plague of locusts in Arabia — my first posting in H.M. Overseas Judiciary — a sharp hurricane in Western Polynesia, a minor earthquake on the Vatuan archipelago and an electrical storm over the Savage Isles. A law for all seasons, if ever there was one. Which is why, with heathenish superstition, I recently included it in my excess baggage upon my return journey to England.

I had been ordered to take a year's medical leave in the U.K. It was a normal sabbatical for anyone who had served more than ten years in curious climates and conditions.

Once here, the bureaucratic process took me over.

'Kindly report at once to your Department of Health Office,' said the letter awaiting me on the hall floor. I did as I was told.

'Fill out the form,' said the irascible gentleman at the desk. I took it into the corner of the crowded room.

'Name of Last Employer?' it demanded right at the top. 'Queen Fatu Hova V of the Savage Islands,' I began to write. She is the reigning granddaughter of the Monarch who had ceded the islands to Britain in the first place.

Then I remembered. A straightforward answer on those lines had almost landed me in the nick a few years before. On holiday from the South Seas, I had been staying in North Wales. Constable Evan Griffiths was doing a routine check on motorists passing through his village one night. I had no driving licence with me. 'Occupation?' he asked, notebook at the ready.

'Lord Chief Justice of the Savage Isles,' I replied, 'and Master of the Rolls, Sabusabu.'

'Well I'm twice as savage, boyo,' came the reply. 'Any

more of your jokes and we'll see how good you are at rolling in the cells!'

'They're both British Protectorates in the South Pacific,' I explained. 'Sabusabu still has the old English title for its Court of Appeal President, which is me.'

Constable Evans calmed down and apologised. He was really a very nice man.

This was clearly not so with the gentleman at the Health Office desk. He was already barking at another client, reading back the entries on his form very loudly and crossly. 'Bound to provoke a seizure,' I decided, and struck out my answer. Playing for safety I wrote instead, 'H.M.G.'

'Won't do at all,' snapped the gentleman at the desk. 'Complete another form with full details.'

By this time I had lost my place in the queue again. I wandered along to the bookstall next door for a breather. There was a huge display on view. *Confessions of a Driving Instructor, Confessions of a Housewife, Confessions of a Window Cleaner.* Memoirs were obviously doing well this year.

I crossed the road to the Reading Room of the Public Library and took out my form. I puzzled over it again without success. Idly I turned it over and began to scribble on the back. 'Confessions of a Judge' I found I'd written.

'Might as well spend the year writing a book like everyone else', I decided. 'At least it puts off going back with the form.'

By the time the book was finished I was fit again. So there was no need to return to the Department of Health Office after all.

Chapter Two

The Shadow of Mungo

'If you're going out *there*,' warned the Manager at the Tropical Outfitters in London, 'you'll still need a pith helmet.' A junior barrister, I was off to the deserts and date palms of British Arabia, to begin my career on the Overseas Bench. Little did I know then that I was to end up among the coconut groves of the South Seas.

'The Kipling,' he called, toppling a large white dome from its cobwebbed sanctuary. He trapped it firmly under one arm and descended the shop ladder with care. 'The finest in pith helmets,' he said, 'steel-lined and fully ventilated.'

I crunched it into position.

'Does it always come so low over the eyes?' I demanded of a tailor's dummy alongside. 'Try pulling it down at the back,' suggested a sales assistant.

'Must be the wrong size,' I complained.

The Manager came to my assistance.

'We don't want to be a figure of fun before the Bedouin, do we, Sir,' he reproved, swivelling the helmet the right way round.

'If you don't mind,' I decided, 'I'll just take the insect-proof trunk for my books.'

With all the enthusiasm of a young lawyer I gave pride of space to my safari law library. Alongside Halsbury, I stuffed in my wig and gown and a pair of shorts, before embarking at Southampton for the long journey through the Mediterranean and the Red Sea.

'The Law of England,' I read in Halsbury, 'is a seasoned traveller.' I was about to turn the page when our Union Steamship liner pitched and rolled again. Even my knuckles were green.

'You can't spend the whole voyage on that bunk,' complained my cabin mate, a hearty tea-planter returning to

Ceylon. 'Anyway, I've entered your name for the deck-quoits competition,' he said. 'Mixed foursomes. So you'll have to snap out of it.'

Obediently I put down Halsbury and tottered after him up to the sports deck.

My partner in the game was a big red lady called Mrs. Stubley.

'I seem to be a long time finding my sea-legs,' I explained. I was a fool to draw attention to my legs. Even though my new drill shorts came down well over the knees, the absence of muscle in the calves, and the deathly white appearance, was startling.

'Try to concentrate on the game,' said my partner. I muffed another shot.

'You'll need a stronger arm than that,' said Mrs. Stubley, 'if you're hoping to keep law and order in Arabia.'

It emerged that her late husband, Mungo Stubley, KC, had been a British Judicial Commissioner in the Middle East. Mungo Stubley had been something of a legend in his day.

'Here goes,' I said. I put everything I'd got into my last throw. The quoit flew right overboard.

'What a stupid way to lose us the game,' said Mrs. Stubley. She stalked back to her deckchair on the foredeck.

'Would you care for a drink, Mrs. Stubley?' I asked. She put down her embroidery.

'You'll have to give that up for a start,' she said. I wiped my steaming brow. 'I was only thinking of half a shandy,' I said.

'Alcohol is strictly forbidden in decent Arab society,' said Mrs. Stubley. 'Mungo considered it our duty to set the same example. 'The natives are always watching us,' he used to say.'

She took a pack of chocolate biscuits from her Dubai travelling bag.

'If you're passing D Deck on your way down,' she said, 'you can drop these in for Basil.'

I hadn't realised that Mrs. Stubley's son was travelling with her.

'How old is the little chap?' I inquired.

'Basil is not little by any standards,' said Mrs. Stubley.

'He's an Alsatian. And you'll find him in the Quarantine Kennels.'

I lost my way twice. They were helpful in the Boiler Room. But my reception in the Beauty Salon was very frosty. Ultimately the sound of barking led me to my destination.

'We've had to put him in a cage of his own,' said the Kennel Steward, when I asked for Mrs. Mungo's pet. 'Unless you want to risk your hand, you'd better leave these with me.'

I handed over the biscuits and hurried away.

Back in my cabin I returned to Halsbury's *Laws of England.*

'English law abroad,' I read, 'has been a settling influence.'

The cabin ceiling was moving again. 'Could do with a settling influence,' I thought, overhearing my tortured stomach. 'Might as well see if I can get some lunch down.'

Luckily there was a stout mahogany rail right along the companion way to the Dining Room.

'Ah there you are,' called Mrs. Stubley. She was towering over the cold-buffet. 'It's bridge this afternoon,' she announced. I toyed uneasily with my bowl of consommé.

'Never quite got the hang of bridge,' I explained. Mrs. Stubley snapped at a piece of celery.

'What about a round of Monopoly?' I suggested. Mrs. Stubley winced.

'If an officer can't play bridge, he shouldn't be in the Service, was what Mungo always maintained,' she said.

Time however lay heavily on her hands, so the following afternoon she condescended to play. I had found a quiet spot amidships. The conservatory, they said, was directly above the stabilisers. Framed in Australian spider-lilies and a Mexican cactus, Mrs. Stubley advised me about my future career, as I set out the board.

'You'll have to deal with a lot of feuding between Arabian tribes from time to time,' she observed, taking over the Chance cards which I had been trying to shuffle. 'That's when they may try to assassinate you.'

I gave the dice in my egg-cup a cowardly rattle.

'Blast,' I said, counting out my score, 'Now I've landed in JAIL.'

'At least you'll be safe there,' commented Mrs. Stubley, with something of a sneer, I thought.

7

I pulled myself together and was about to erect a cheap hotel at Islington when the bells rang for Life Boat Drill.

We were both assigned to the same lifeboat. The Purser was in charge of our particular group.

'A couple of volunteers please,' he called. Mrs. Stubley was already there. She beckoned in my direction. I came out from behind the bulwark and the other passengers parted to let me through.

'Your husband's looking a bit shaky on his pins,' said the Purser, 'but he'll do.'

Mrs. Stubley decided to ignore this insult to the dead. With a grim smile she pushed me ahead of her into the lifeboat and then clambered aboard herself.

'Are you a good swimmer?' she inquired as the boat swayed on its davits down towards the water.

'Only at the shallow end,' I replied. It looked as though it might have to be the deep one this time, because the boat was now tipping dangerously to Mrs. Stubley's side. I tried to hitch the lifebelt closer around me.

'Mungo was a swimming blue,' observed Mrs. Stubley.

A jolt to the right of me made me open my eyes. The Purser had joined us.

'A bit of ballast needed on your side,' he laughed.

To the cheers of the rest of our group we returned safely to the deck.

It was a relief to get back to the seclusion of the Monopoly table. I drew a card 'PAY THE DOCTOR £50'.

'Not many doctors where you're going,' warned Mrs. Stubley. 'Self-reliance was Mungo's motto.' She paused to check that I had paid out the correct money to the Bank. 'Know the answer to a scorpion's bite, for instance,' she asked.

'I don't think the question came up in the Bar Finals,' I chaffed.

Mrs. Stubley advanced sternly to Go.

'It would soon wipe that smile off your face if you suffered one,' she reprimanded.

I took my next turn, only to land on the Water Works already owned by my opponent.

'Water,' said Mrs. Stubley. 'Always in short supply in Arabia.' She took a bonus from the Community Chest. 'Mungo could go without a drop of water for two days provided he was wearing a pith helmet.'

I sipped at my lemonade. Perhaps I should have heeded the Manager's advice at the Tropical Outfitters in London, I thought.

I turned my attention back to the game. 'Here goes,' I called, trying hard for a double six. My score was two. 'I seem to be on Park Lane,' I said. Mrs. Stubley held out her hand. 'Which means you owe me £1200 rent,' she declared. That was the end of the match.

We had bright weather across the rest of the Mediterranean, but I maintained a dim record at our daily Monopoly sessions.

'I'll be leaving you here,' announced Mrs. Stubley when our ship docked at Port Said. Apparently she now lived in a bungalow at Alexandria.

I felt duty bound to escort her ashore. Basil came with us.

'Mrs. Stubley,' I called down the gangway. 'I don't think Basil wants to be friends.' His nostrils were already distended.

'He doesn't like your rolled umbrella,' laughed Mrs. Stubley, calling the brute to heel. 'Mungo always carried a sword-stick.'

It was heavy going along the wharf with one of Mrs. Stubley's portmanteaus in each hand. 'The porters here demand such outrageous tips,' she complained.

She pointed towards the customers' Car Park behind Simon Artz, the famous tourist gift-store.

'I parked my little runabout in there,' she said.

I was surprised to find her Austin 7 still intact. Even in Egypt, it seemed, nobody dared to steal from Mrs. Stubley.

She and Basil forced their way inside, along with the portmanteaus.

'The battery's flat,' said Mrs. Stubley. This was hardly surprising since she'd been away in England for three months.

'Give me a push from the back,' she ordered. She and Basil watched my futile efforts to get the vehicle in motion.

'Mungo could have lifted a car this size,' said Mrs. Stubley.

At last the engine jerked into life. She and Basil poked their heads through the window. I made my farewell.

'Not a patch on Mungo,' I heard one of them murmur, as they drove away.

Chapter Three

Prisoner's Aid

My own little port of disembarkation lay 400 miles south of Port Said, on the shores of the Red Sea. 'Fort Allambra', in the Township of Sheikh Suliman, according to my letter of appointment, was to be my official residence. It sounded exotic.

I managed to charter a desert taxi to take me there. Names like Lawrence, Wolseley and Gordon, flashed through my mind as we bumped over the sand. 'That'll be it,' I thought, as an impressive blue domed edifice, with a flag on top, came into view. However the taxi-driver drew up beside a pile of rubble on the other side of the Maidan.

'I've paid to be taken right up to Fort Allambra,' I protested.

'This is him,' he replied.

He helped me out with my belongings. The imposing blue building opposite turned out to be the shrine of a local saint. 'Fort Allambra' had been severely bombarded by the Turks during the First World War. Behind the rubble I was relieved to discover that the Commandant's dwelling, a plain whitewashed building, was still intact. This was where I set up home.

From Fort Allambra it took me less than five minutes to walk to my courthouse in Sheikh Suliman. It was an extension of the bazaar. Along its sandblown verandahs squatted sellers of roasted corn and sweet-meats, fishmongers and goat dealers. Customers crowded the rails when I arrived on my inaugural day.

A stout man in a black fez awaited me at the top of the main steps. He was bellowing loudly in Arabic and flailing the air with a flat scourge.

'I,' he announced angrily, 'am Bhindi, Clerk of Court. And these,' he added, indicating a rustling cloud of insects above his head, 'is bloody great plague of locusts.'

Mr Bhindi rasped a few words of command and the Court Usher gathered my trunk of law books from the taxi. 'Follow please,' said Mr Bhindi.

It was difficult to feel at home in the District Judge's Chambers, where Mr Bhindi conducted me. This was partly because of the locusts. Giant armoured creatures, like flying prawns, they seemed to be everywhere, on desks, tables, chairs. It was lucky that I had with me my trunk of law books.

Whether Lord Chancellor Halsbury in sponsoring such a weighty edition of the *Laws of England* had the execution of locusts in mind is not known. But scattered from a height by Mr Bhindi, the usher and myself, volumes one to twelve proved effective. With the locusts out of the way, judicial work could at last begin.

'Silence,' called Mr Bhindi, opening the door which led from my chambers into the crowded court-room. I took my seat on a sagging green platform under the punkah.

'Applications,' called Mr Bhindi settling comfortably below.

A party of Bedouin shepherds, skins tinged with indigo, sharp daggers at their waists, trooped in. They wanted a summons against a fraudulent moneylender. Next came a family of camel-traders. They had to record a contract in the Register kept by the court for this purpose. Mr Bhindi obtained the necessary thumb prints before turning to the Criminal Register.

'Fifteen riots,' he explained, handing up a sheaf of charge sheets. I almost lost half the charge sheets in the hot wind that blew in like the blast from a furnace. However, I was able to dispose rapidly of the riot cases, all the defendants having escaped over the frontier into Saudi Arabia. We turned to the rest of the morning cases.

Some of the cases in the list on that day, and on many days that followed, reminded me of courts in England. The smells outside were different — goats, coffee, spices, and woodsmoke instead of fish and chips and diesel fumes. But the pattern of crime was alike — burglaries committed by teenagers, thefts from marketstalls committed by women, as with English shoplifting.

12

Comparisons like these made the setting a little less strange. But then an incident would shatter all such attempts at familiarization. Like the day the prisoner jumped into the sea.

It was not my fault so much as Mr Mukerjee's. Mr Mukerjee was a shirtmaker whose sign 'King Farouk's Own Lucky Tailor Man' had caught my eye on an early shopping visit to the bazaar. For my court appearances I had decided something more formal was required than the linen ducks which I had worn in the evening on the sea voyage. After several conferences with Mr Mukerjee, in a curtained alcove lined with faded pictures of English sahibs in plus-fours and yachting caps, the 'District Judge's Suit' was delivered to me wrapped in the pages of a revolutionary Arab newspaper. It was intended to be an equatorial version of the English barrister's dark suit. But in the harsh sunlight of Arabia the black alpaca chosen by Mr Mukerjee had an ominous gleam. It shone like gravestone marble. The shoulders, too, were oddly rucked, giving an almost hunchback effect. Perhaps the final touch was the patch I was obliged to wear over one eye due to an optical heat infection which developed soon after my arrival.

Whatever it was, the first prisoner on that particular morning, a small wrinkled Yemeni charged with a passport offence, took one look at me and dived out of the dock. In a flash, before the warders could lay hands on him, he was out on the verandah and plunging down into the shark-infested waters which lapped the stone parapet. Surrounded by excited litigants and lawyers, I watched him bob slowly out across the water, making for the far side of the estuary at least a mile away. A police launch followed out in hot pursuit and he was soon brought back by the warders, forlorn and dripping in the dock.

'Prisoner has to be deported,' explained Mr Bhindi. I made the necessary order.

'He'll need a change of clothing for the journey,' I pointed out. I adjourned eagerly to chambers.

I believe Mr Mukerjee's Suit became something of an attraction in the fairgrounds of the Yemen. For myself, I was only too pleased to hand over this dread symbol of Imperial Power.

Chapter Four

In the Chair

'So,' hissed my first caller of the following morning, 'Your Honour is having no use for my fine Judge's Suit.' It was King Farouk's Own Lucky Tailor Man.

'An act of charity,' I told him. Despite much patient explanation on my part, he was inconsolable. 'All right, Mr Lucky,' I said at last, 'I'll buy something from you off the peg, instead.'

He was back in a trice with the flowing white robes of a Tribal Emir on his arm.

'All very well for Lawrence of Arabia,' I said, 'but not for me I'm afraid.'

By now he had the floor of my chambers covered with a variety of desert headdresses.

'Mr Lucky,' I said, 'these chambers are not the headquarters of the French Foreign Legion.'

'I'll just take this turban,' I said. 'Use it as a cummerbund.'

Mr Lucky immediately burst into tears.

'Do pull yourself together,' I protested, handing him my handkerchief.

'I make tip-top jacket in cream sharkskin,' he blubbed.

I had not, until then, pictured myself looking like Humphrey Bogart in *Casablanca*.

'Anything,' I decided, to get the emotional tailorman to dry his eyes.

'Sorry about the late start,' I explained to Mr Bhindi, having placed my order and escaped into court. The Clerk lifted his fez, bowed curtly, and began to rattle through the day's cases at an impossible speed.

'Drunk in charge of a Donkey Cart Contrary to Section Sixty-seven of Traffic Act, Watering Goat Milk for Sale Contrary to Section Fourteen of Food Act, Desecration of Holy Tomb Contrary to Section Thirty-eight Burial Laws

Amendment Act, Counterfeiting Marie Thérèse Dollars Contrary to Coining Act, Beating Carpets in the Street Punishable under Street Offenders Act, Theft of Water Contrary to Irrigation Regulations Schedule Two.' He paused for breath. The dock was now jammed with defendants.

Mr Bhindi stabbed a podgy forefinger in the direction of the inebriated muleteer.

'Guilty or Not Guilty?' he demanded.

There followed a heated exchange in Arabic.

'He says he's not guilty,' reported Mr Bhindi.

The defendant hiccuped alarmingly.

'Perhaps he hasn't understood you, Mr Bhindi,' I said. The Clerk shook his head.

'Well, it's exceedingly difficult even for me to follow you,' I complained. 'And for my part,' I added with a touch of asperity, 'I'm as sober as a judge.'

As I spoke, the defendant fell back into the arms of the Court Usher. So we put his case back until the end of the day. This at least meant he could sleep off the disastrous effects of his toddy-drinking in the cells.

I fined the fraudulent milkman, and began the hearing of the Burial Act offence. The accused was a wandering Yafei musician, clad in a shabby white chemise with a sash of threadbare red velvet across his right shoulder.

'Arrested while cooking his supper on the tomb of Saint Sayid Hashid,' declared Mr Bhindi.

The musician sucked mournfully on an empty tobacco pipe, fashioned out of a used cartridge shell.

'How could he tell it was a tomb?' I inquired.

'Everybody knows that,' said Mr Bhindi.

'I ought to see for myself,' I persisted.

I adjourned to look at the site. This meant a ten-minute walk in the broiling sun.

'Should have taken one of those headdresses from Mr Lucky after all,' I reflected.

The tomb was on the very edge of the township, partially hidden under a tuft of wild palms. We pitched an informal camp in the meagre shade.

I turned to speak to the defendant. He was about to take a quiet nap against a sand dune.

16

'Did you come here by night?' I asked. The old musician nodded. 'I suppose we could return at sunset,' I began, then caught sight of the expression on Mr Bhindi's face.

I moved away to examine the cairn of limestone. I was pretty certain that in darkness no visitor could have recognised it for what it was.

'Case dismissed,' I ruled.

'And the blessings of Saint Sayid will follow you all your days,' declared the old man.

There was certainly no evidence of any saintly assistance with my labours of the rest of the day.

Abdulla, the water thief, who wore a calico skull-cap and a broad grin throughout the proceedings, was a particular problem. Nobody had been able to understand why his strip of land produced twice the normal crop of melons.

'The Will of Allah,' he had always claimed.

His cunning was now exposed. He had constructed an underground channel to feed his crop between the bottom of the Public Irrigation Channel and the bed of the Sheikh Suliman stream.

'Twenty sacks of melons to be forfeited,' I decreed. Abdullah's gold teeth glinted in the sun.

'And one for your Lordship, maybe,' he murmured. I treated this flagrant insinuation of corruption with short shrift.

'I don't like melons,' I said.

The carpet-beater found me in more temperate mood.

'A conditional discharge,' I decreed, before turning to the last case of the morning.

'Guilty with extenuating circumstances,' explained Mr Joshi the counterfeit artist. His English was as impeccable as his dress. A Bombay silversmith by origin, he had travelled widely and expensively.

The Marie Thérèse dollars which Mr Joshi had fraudulently reproduced in his private mint were still the common currency of South Arabia. Dutch traders of the eighteenth century had first introduced the coins into the country. Holland was part of the Holy Roman Empire, so the coins bore the curvaceous effigy of the Holy Roman Empress.

The 'extenuating circumstances' proved to be the demands of Mr Joshi's creditors. Mr Joshi had a long record of fraud, including many convictions in India for counterfeiting. I put off sentencing in his case, so that the police inspector could obtain more details of his past.

'Wise sentencing is the mark of a good judge.' This was the oft-repeated mot of the Learned Bencher who had finally sanctioned my call to the Bar.

'I'd like to see him getting the scales right under these sort of pressures.' I remember thinking.

In some cases, imprisonment was unfortunately the only proper sentence. This turned out to be so with Mr Joshi.

But sending the defendant to prison was not always the end of the matter, as I discovered on an early visit to the barbers.

'British hair cut?' inquired the proprietor as I stood hesitantly under his sign, 'High Society Saloon', at the corner of the Suk.

'Just a trim,' I decided. The saloon keeper guided me past several chickens into the vacant chair.

'Cheap at any price,' he declared. He was referring to the haircut, not to the chair, from which one spring protruded even more savagely than the other. This set me at a quaint angle, but since the cracked mirror on the wall was similarly inclined, vision, at least, was not inconvenienced.

'What hairstyle are you wanting?' asked my host, handing me some curry-stained photographs of Rudolph Valentino, Lloyd George and ex-King Carol of Rumania.

'Finish,' he interrupted, tired of my indecision. 'I give light crop.'

He tucked a piece of gunny bag about me.

'No damn hairs running down the body,' he explained. From under his turban he produced an elderly pair of scissors and set to work.

'Big job this,' complained the barber after a while. He was snorting horribly, like a boxer. 'Ali,' he yelled. A shrivelled brown acolyte appeared from behind the curtain. 'Bring clippers.' These were kept in a glass case by the door. His mission fulfilled, Ali stood by, twitching admiringly. 'Thinning out,' instructed the craftsman. He now had the clipper-gears hopelessly enmeshed in my hair. 'Needing a bit of oil,' he observed, hurrying outside.

It was a long wait, especially with the clippers suspended

from my locks. Ali lit a joss stick to keep back the flies. His master returned at last. 'Bob your uncle,' he proclaimed, emptying a jar of Macassar oil over me. By twisting forward I could glimpse his handiwork in the looking-glass. I had been given a fringe like Henry V at Agincourt. 'Good job,' smirked the hairstylist behind me.

'How's about a nose-cut?' he inquired, pointing to his own hirsute nostrils. I shook my battered head. 'Righty,' he countered, 'I give free massage.' Before I could decline, he was already grinding his knuckles into my scalp.

'You Government fellow?' whispered Ali sympathetically. By this time the Maître had begun to shave my neck with a sharp knife.

'District Judge,' I rejoined. My face received an even closer inspection.

'You Judge Overton?' exclaimed the barber. I nodded, flattered by recognition. 'My brother knows you,' he mused, scraping away near my jugular. 'You send him to prison last week.' I held firmly to the sides of the chair. The hairdresser took another mouthful of red betel-nut. 'You very hard man,' he announced, baring his crimson teeth.

'I'd prefer not to discuss the case,' I said, levering myself up out of the chair. The helpful Ali began to dust my jacket with a piece of rag, but his employer was not to be deterred.

'My brother,' he declared, 'he got two wifes and seventeen childrens.' He patted his ample stomach. 'And I got the hunger with keeping them.'

Other customers were gathering around with interest.

'I'm sorry about that,' I said, 'but I'm afraid your brother's case was a bad one. He had a great number of previous convictions and not one of those watches he received has been recovered.'

I paid the barber his fee together with a tip. He was still not satisfied.

'You like to buy hair tonic,' he insisted, indicating several bottles of vivid green elixir at the back of a showcase.

'Oh, very well,' I agreed wearily.

This mollified him. He put his arm into the case and in doing so pulled back his grimy cuff. By a strange coincidence he had a brand new watch on his wrist.

Mere suspicion, as English judges have so frequently

explained to juries at home and abroad, has never been enough to justify any conclusion under our law. So there was no aftermath to my visit to that particular barber. And yet the incident was a pointer to some of the other strange happenings I was to encounter overseas. 'It is not,' reported an English Parliamentary Committee, 'from the judges that the most accurate and satisfactory evidence of the effect of the English criminal law can reasonably be expected. They only see the exterior of criminal proceedings after they are brought into a court of justice. Of the cases that never appear there, and of the causes that prevent their appearance they can know nothing. Of the motives which influence the testimony of witnesses, they can form but a hasty and inadequate estimate. Even in the grounds of verdicts, they may often be deceived. From many opportunities of observing the influence of punishment upon those men among whom malefactors are most commonly found, they are by their duties, placed at a great distance.'

Beginning perhaps with my visit to the Arabian hairdresser, my own experience as a judge was not to be quite as the English Parliamentary Committee had suggested. There was less of the 'great distance' than imagined, and sometimes, it seemed, none at all.

Chapter Five

Mr Bhindi's Bargain

'What exactly are they doing here?' I asked Mr Bhindi a few weeks later. I had come into Sheikh Suliman Domestic Court to find a couple of camels tethered to the witness stand.

'They're mine,' said Mr Bhindi. Mr Bhindi's steel-rimmed spectacles concealed a remarkably sharp eye for profit and the camels were apparently just another of his bargains.

'Please remove them,' I said, adding with weary irony, 'domestic proceedings are *supposed* to be held in camera.'

Mr Bhindi reluctantly led them to the palm trees beyond the verandah, where a number of Arab wives, veiled in black, were waiting for him to call their domestic cases for hearing.

In domestic cases, Mohammedan, not English, law applied. This was because it was so bound up with the religion of the country as laid down by the Prophet Mahommed.

Mohammedan law allowed the husband to divorce his wife merely by saying the word *talak* (I dismiss) three times. The wife, however, had no such right. I was always complaining to Mr Bhindi of the Mohammedan law's unfairness to women and about their lack of compensation, but he would never agree.

'You must not forget the deferred *mahr*,' he used to say. *Mahr* means dowry. Under Mohammedan law the wife was supposed to get the deferred *mahr* upon divorce.

'The law of *mahr* is all part of the marriage bargain,' he emphasised, 'Thus our Prophet made the law also fair to women.'

Poor Mr Bhindi. The Mohammedan law of *mahr* was to be his downfall.

It was Mr Bhindi's custom in the cool of the day to walk up the wadi, working out his latest profits as he went. He usually wore a faded Bedouin skirt tightly knotted over his plump behind and short fat legs. Returning from his walk one evening, he caught sight of Fatima, daughter of Qadhi Hassan unveiled in her father's date garden.

'Of highest value,' he confided to me next morning. 'Like a pearl from Kuwait.'

I pictured Mr Bhindi restless in his frugal bachelor retreat. Wakeful at the first glimmer of dawn, he must have listened distractedly to the Muhsin calling the faithful to prayer from the minaret below his house, until Aboker, the cook, shuffled in with a glass of coffee. This was always, I knew, an irritating reminder to him of the extravagance of paying a servant. Sipping his coffee upon one such morning Mr Bhindi solved his problem.

'By marrying Fatima, I can do without Aboker,' he explained to me. I agreed to act as an intermediary to arrange the marriage. I spoke to Qadhi Hassan upon Mr Bhindi's behalf. The reply was not unfavourable and we were invited to call together at the Qadhi's house on the outskirts of the town. We found the Qadhi sitting over his books and manuscripts, their ink brown with age. No mention was made of the purpose of our visit.

A pleasant smell of roasting meat floated over the verandah.

'Pray eat with us,' said the Qadhi. Cooked rice was brought in baskets, a table-cloth was laid, dates, bread and honey were spread upon it. The marriage could not be discussed until the meal was over. In fact the Qadhi refrained from mentioning his daughter's *mahr* until we were leaving.

'It will be but twenty-five camels and 2,000 Marie Thérèse dollars,' he murmured.

'Out of the question,' snapped Mr Bhindi. And so, for a while, the matter rested.

It was during the brief rains, when the wadi was flooded with water, that he next saw Fatima.

'She was bathing behind a tamarisk bush,' he recounted. Unfortunately for Mr Bhindi it transpired that Fatima was perfect in figure. He begged me to re-open discussions as to her bride-price.

23

After considerable bargaining Mr Bhindi's two camels were accepted as a down payment of *mahr*, with the remainder deferred and to be paid over ten years. They clasped hands.

'There are also the wedding expenses,' the Qadhi hinted. 'Just a ring, candles, sweetmeats, bed and bed coverings. Say two shifts, one of crimson silk, the other of blue cotton, two veils, two pairs of shagreen slippers, four chains for the neck hung with bells, and six gold bracelets. As for the singers and musicians and the cost of the feast — 500 dollars at the most.'

Negotiations were again broken off.

Mr Bhindi tried cold baths. He avoided the wadi. It was no use. I could see that an unquenchable passion had been aroused in the portly registrar of Sheikh Suliman court. Upon his behalf I sent a message to Qadhi Hassan that Mr Bhindi would pay what was demanded.

I witnessed the marriage contract, which the Qadhi sealed with his gold signet ring. The wedding was fixed. It was celebrated on the day after Ramadan and I was privileged to attend.

Mr Bhindi sat on a special mound of carpets, with the Qadhi clicking his rosaries nearby. The hubble-bubble was passed around. Eventually the Qadhi led the way to another room. A latticed door opened onto the bride, cross-legged on the marriage couch. She was encased in rich draperies, her face hidden by veils. Mr Bhindi was placed in the bridegroom's position with the male relations in the opposite corner of the room. The music began. The ensuing feast was lavish and interminable. At last we guests bade the happy couple good-night.

It was traditional among the people of Sheikh Suliman for the bridegroom to take to the marriage-bed first. His clothes had then to be removed by his wife. Custom finally decreed that the bride must resign her veil before extinguishing the light.

I believe it was at this moment that Mr Bhindi let out a stream of unseemly oaths. Seconds later, so the servants told me, his naked and indignant figure streaked across Qadhi Hassan's courtyard. Mr Bhindi hammered in vain at the Qadhi's door.

'A great fraud, a great fraud,' he cried unheard into the desert air.

Mr Bhindi and the Qadhi were waiting for me when I arrived at court later that morning.

'You have my daughter, Mr Bhindi,' the Qadhi was saying. 'Of what do you complain?'

'Yes,' shrieked Mr Bhindi, 'but which damn daughter — the eldest and plainest of the lot!'

The Qadhi laid a soothing hand upon his shoulder, and turned to me.

'I stipulated my daughter,' he answered, 'but not which one.'

Mr Bhindi ground his teeth.

'I will divorce her at once,' he warned. I took out a copy of the marriage contract.

'In that event, Mr Bhindi,' I interposed, 'you must pay the balance of *mahr* — nineteen more camels and 2,000 dollars immediately.'

Mr Bhindi knew he was beaten. With sullen grace he resigned himself to returning to the bridal home.

'All part of the bargain, Mr Bhindi,' I reminded him. 'As you always said, thus the Prophet made the law fair to women.'

That was the only laugh I ever had at Mr Bhindi's expense. More often, as we shall see, it was the other way around.

Chapter Six

By Official Transport

'Is official transport provided?' I inquired of Mr Bhindi some months afterwards. I was required the following day to hold court at Alkazir on the other side of the Sheikh Suliman estuary. Mr Bhindi shook his head.

'But I have great bargain motor for your special hire,' he said.

'Thank you, Mr Bhindi,' I said warily, 'but I feel sure I can borrow my neighbour's.'

'Done it!' I congratulated myself after an early start for Alkazir next morning in the borrowed car. I had safely forded the estuary at low tide. I spoke too soon. I had proceeded only a short distance along the track on the other side when, with a tell-tale splutter, the neighbour's motor seized up. After a long wait by the roadside I was thankful to see a lorry coming up behind me. It proved to be a curious vehicle with a sort of bamboo cage on the back. The tiny cab in front was only just big enough for the driver, a grim looking official in a dark-blue uniform.

'I simply must get to Alkazir by 10.00 am,' I explained, after waving him to a shaky halt. He jerked a thumb at the rising waters of the estuary.

'No more traffic this morning,' he replied, 'high tide starting.' I glanced inquiringly at the rear accommodation of his own vehicle. 'You not like travelling with my passenger in there,' he said.

'What are you carrying,' I joked, 'a captured lion?'

'A captured prisoner,' he answered sternly, 'I take him to court at Alkazir for trial.'

A ridiculous quandary. If I let the lorry go on without me there would be no trial.

With considerable misgiving I finally decided to conceal my identity and risk a ride in the cage. Squeezing inside was not easy either, because of the size of my travelling companion, a tattooed Somali of frightening girth.

'Nice of you to give me a lift,' I began, but the poor fellow made it clear — by a somewhat embarrassing gesture — that he was in no mood for pleasantries.

We bumped along to our destination in silent discomfort.

Just as we were turning into the Court House compound we ran over a goat. Our driver immediately entered into a passionate argument with the owner of the goat and completely forgot about me.

I shook and hammered the padlocked door of the cage, only to cover myself with oily rust and sand. Eventually a constable put his head out of the Court House.

'If you don't keep quiet in there,' he shouted, 'I'll bring the Judge to you.'

'That won't be necessary,' I called back, 'he's already here!'

I think the police officer may have recognized a hint of authority in my voice because he soon came along to release me.

'Would you like me to clean you up, sir?' he simpered.

I was silly to wear my cream sharkskin that day. It was even sillier to hand it over to the policeman. I don't know exactly what he did to it, but no brawl in *Casablanca*, however violent, had ever left Humphrey Bogart's jacket in such a condition.

Worse still, Mr Bhindi had arrived at Alkazir before me and was now savouring my embarrassment from the steps of the Court House.

'I see your Honour obtained Official Transport after all,' he smirked.

'At least I'm here on time, Mr Bhindi,' I snapped, striding stiffly past him into court.

The case involving the Somali was the last of the day.

'I believe you have already met the Judge,' observed Mr Bhindi to the giant felon. To my consternation the unhappy man merely repeated the unseemly gesture with which he had earlier greeted me. Fortunately his trial proved a short one. He pleaded guilty to escaping from lawful custody. My only duty was to impose the necessary prison sentence.

Rather stupidly, however, I left the court without explaining to the prisoner that he could appeal against my sentence if he wished.

'Just ask the warder to take the prisoner along to my chambers,' I said to Mr Bhindi. 'I can explain to him in there.' Mr Bhindi turned upon his heel with a chuckle. 'May we share the joke, Mr Bhindi?' I interjected sharply.

'Just tickled by a thought,' he replied. 'If Your Honour also travelled back together, you could explain to him yourself on the way.'

Chapter Seven

The Daily Routine

'I'm God,' snapped the defendant in answer to the charge of common assault.

'Then no doubt you'll be pleading not guilty,' I observed. Mr Bhindi said nothing. As the years passed by in Sheikh Suliman Court he showed himself increasingly indifferent to my problems.

The defendant wore a red beard and a blanket. He settled back in the dock with Olympian detachment as the evidence against him was called.

It transpired that he had been distributing private tracts outside the mosque. He claimed to be the New Messiah. The complainant, a devout fisherman, had challenged this assertion. The defendant assaulted the fisherman. Hence the proceedings before me.

'Does the accused wish to give testimony on — er — divine oath?' I inquired of the interpreter.

'Certainly not,' came the reply.

I bound the Almighty over. He shook hands all round and departed, taking with him, I learnt later, the warder's new boots.

The remaining cases from the bazaar that day were more humdrum; the usual bevy of stall-holders sued for debt.

The Debtors' Prison was a little shuttered house on the outskirts of the settlement. It was run by an enterprising lodging-house keeper. The cost of boarding the inmates had to be met by the creditors themselves.

'Why, Mr Yahooda,' I once asked a prosperous money-lender, 'do you insist upon the defendant's going to prison?' I suggested that he would find it cheaper to allow his debtor to carry on working. 'At least he might earn something to repay you,' I pointed out.

31

Mr Yahooda was adamant. He made away with his client to the Debtors' Prison.

Back came Mr Yahooda a few weeks later asking for the prisoner to be released. 'That riff-raff fellow,' he sobbed, 'his belly's got so fat on rice I am paying for, he now ask for new clothes to fit him!' Mr Yahooda would have welcomed the law of Ancient Rome which permitted a creditor to cut out a piece of the debtor's stomach.

The construction of a vast new oil refinery across the estuary from Sheikh Suliman gave me a busy time as judge of the Workmen's Compensation Court. Abdulla, a Yemeni tribesman, who had come across the desert frontier to sign on for the construction company, would injure himself at work. The tariff of compensation under our Workmen's Compensation Act — say 500 rupees for the loss of Abdulla's little finger — was a system widely recognised by many ancient laws. In AD 605 King Ethelbert awarded three shillings for the loss of a thumb-nail. I had always been irritated by King Ine of Wessex, AD 700. For knocking off a Welsh or Scots man he prescribed half the compensation given for killing a Saxon. King Alfred preferred to distinguish between the sexes. He ordered twice the amount for violence to a man as he did for violence to a woman.

Mr Bhindi would have agreed with King Alfred. So would most of the male community in Sheikh Suliman.

'Why,' I demanded one afternoon of Ali, a mild little watchmaker from the Suk, 'did you beat your wife?'

'Because she went to the football match,' he answered. The explanation struck me as inadequate.

'Well,' came the patient explanation through the interpreter, 'all the other women who went with her have been punished by their husbands. Many have also been divorced, but I have been merciful.'

A popular team of Egyptian footballers had visited the town. Some of the more intrepid wives had ventured from their purdah quarters to peep at the game. Caught *in flagrante delicto* they had been severely dealt with by outraged husbands. Unfortunately, Ali had been seen setting about his spouse by a government official. This led to his appearance in court and a sharp fine.

The punishment of the lady football fans reminded me of

32

a law of Ancient Greece. Any woman who crossed the Alpheus to watch the Olympic Games was to be thrown from the top of Mount Typhaion.

Games, or rather gaming, in the non-Olympian sense, was something else which we tried to control overseas just as in England. Hence the occasion when I tried 134 Chinamen for gaming. Nobody in the Chinese dockland community could understand why. The game was called Fan Tan. They had always played it. 'Why,' they asked themselves, 'should English law forbid it?' However, under the English Gaming Acts, such games of chance were illegal. It was unusual to see any Chinaman in a criminal court, for the Chinese minority was law-abiding. There was no room for the public at the hearing because the defendants filled every nook and cranny.

'A lidiculous tlial,' commented Mr Li Po Lung, defendant number forty-nine, leaping to his tiny feet from his seat upstairs in the gallery. Mr Lung was a restaurant proprietor, respectable and well liked. The evidence against Mr Lung and his 133 companions was clear. They had been playing Fan Tan, and so I had to collect 655 rupees from them. They paid up dutifully, but Mr Lung was by no means the first to question the suitability of certain English laws which we introduced overseas.

The basics of English law and order, the system of courts, our traditions of justice, were not unwelcome. What was queried was the wholesale reception of English law into such different societies. A light meal of the laws of England might be a good thing. It was the seven-course dinner which caused indigestion.

Indigestion, or worse, food-poisoning, was a major issue in a case I tried a year or two later. Mr Hak, owner of the Crescent Night Club, was summonsed under the Public Health Regulations for serving meals from unhygienic kitchens.

'Filthy lies,' he insisted when the charges were put.

'The court will see for itself,' I announced and adjourned the hearing.

At the suggestion of the Public Health Inspector I paid a surprise visit to the Club in the evening.

The lights were all out at the Crescent Night Club when I

arrived. Policemen tussled with an angry crowd of seamen outside.

Most ships bound for the East fuelled at the harbour nearby, so Mr Hak's establishment was popular with sailors of many nationalities or, rather, unpopular on this occasion. The target for their displeasure was Mr Hak, prominent in an off-white dinner jacket.

'Everybody hold horses,' he implored from behind the entrance kiosk.

'Lighting plant gone for the burton,' he confided, smuggling me through a side entrance to a seat near the band.

It was some time before I realised that a shortish lady was peeping at me over the table.

'My wife is saying, "how's tricks",' explained Mr Hak, introducing his other half, or, more accurately, his other quarter. 'Kindly dance her,' decreed my host. Mohammed Abdulla bin Hassam and his Crescent Seven were playing 'Moonglow' as we took to the floor.

Somebody knocked over a hurricane lamp. 'Are you there, Mrs Hak?' I called, having lost her underfoot during the samba.

The electricity came on again. Twelve o'clock came, and with it the cabaret.

'Shufti, my lord,' whispered Mr Hak. 'Shufti my daughters.' He indicated two ladies of the chorus, whose sinister features I had thought familiar. 'They are learning since the cradle,' he said.

Just then the cook emerged from the distinctly whiffy kitchens.

'Give the big hand,' directed Mr Hak. The enterprising menial began a juggling display.

'He'd do well on the British Halls,' I murmured politely.

'We are loving everything British,' enthused Mr Hak, already excessively drunk.

'Steady there, Mr Hak,' I remonstrated. He had me in a damp embrace.

'I am loving you my lord like a blood brother,' Mr Hak persisted. 'Like a bloody brother,' he emphasised with rare affection.

During the enforced absence of the chef, a curry caught alight in the rear annexe. I managed to escape amid the

34

excitement.

The fire obliged Mr Hak to rebuild his kitchens, so I deferred sentence in the case against him to make sure that the new premises and equipment satisfied the Health Inspector.

This also allowed me to forget about Mr Hak for the time being and get on with the many other cases awaiting attention. For in this way at least, court in Arabia was no different from the U.K. The backlog of cases was always on the increase.

'Will you adjourn for lunch?' I recall my neighbour enquiring as I set forth for another busy session.

'Not a hope,' I replied. 'There is bound to be a heavy list.'

I remember that I was able to deal fairly smartly, for one reason or another, with the remands that day. I then embarked upon the first of the trials.

Two Yemeni carpet dealers were charged with illegal possession of a home-made firearm. A cheerful policeman from the border police station produced the firearm.

Mr Tarpawaller, the eighty-year-old doyen of the local Bar, rose shakily to cross-examine. 'Vell,' said Mr Tarpawaller, 'vill it shoot?' The happy policeman looked sad. 'Answer the question. Make for him to answer my question,' insisted Mr Tarpawaller.

'I cannot know, Sir, I have not fired it,' said the policeman.

Mr Tarpawaller threw up his hands. There was a wheezing sound from his throat. Without a word he bowed himself out on to the verandah. He spat into the dust and bowed himself back into court.

'Submission, Your Honour,' he croaked. 'No case to answer, Your Honour, Sir.'

Mr Tarpawaller sat down.

'Just a moment, Mr Tarpawaller,' I said, taking up the firearm. 'This is obviously a trigger.'

It was not so much the deafening sound when it went off as the gaping hole in the roof which disconcerted me. 'A convenient time to adjourn,' I muttered through the swirling dust.

'So,' said my neighbour, a little later, 'you did adjourn for lunch.'

'Not for lunch, just for brandy,' I replied.

Chapter Eight

The Perils of Office

'Votch out,' squeaked Mr Tarpawaller, as I stepped unexpectedly into Sheikh Suliman Court one morning. An earthenware water-pitcher flew past me. Mr Tarpawaller was the thrower, Mr Bhindi the target.

'Really gentlemen,' I expostulated. They were known to quarrel, but this was going too far. 'Mr Tarpawaller,' I said, 'despite your venerable age and seniority, I shall have to bind you over if this sort of thing goes on.'

'Flog him,' interjected Mr Bhindi.

I motioned the enraged octogenarian back to his seat at the Pleaders' Bar.

'Bhindi has refused my application with unforgivable insult,' he quavered.

'Rubbish application,' retorted Mr Bhindi. 'Dead loss contrary to Section 156 Civil Procedure Code.'

Mr Tarpawaller was trying to get to his feet again.

'The learned Clerk has every right to reject an application if procedurally incorrect,' I said.

'But not to stamp his great foot upon it,' complained Mr Tarpawaller. I managed to soothe him down again.

'I shall review the application myself,' I said.

The DOCUMENT OF APPLICATION was still wedged between the thongs of Mr Bhindi's right sandal. He managed to extract it and placed it, somewhat the worse for wear, on the Bench. I had great difficulty in deciphering the unsavoury exhibit.

Mr Tarpawaller was anxious to assist me. 'In my application I am asking Your Honour to review an assessment of rent,' he explained, 'upon one of my own properties.'

'Upon one of his pig-sties,' commented Mr Bhindi.

37

'I am addressing the Master, not his mule,' said Mr Tarpawaller.

Comparison with the lowest of animals in Arabian tradition was too much for Mr Bhindi's pride. With a gesture of rage he reached up and pushed the punka in Mr Tarpawaller's direction. Although a gross contempt of court, his action proved no threat to Mr Tarpawaller. The punkah merely rocketed back on its pulleys and took Mr Bhindi with it. In the collision with my desk, my heavy Victorian wig stand — a parting gift from Mother — shot off sideways and caught me a nasty crack on the knee.

'You're suspended from duty, Mr Bhindi,' I called. Even my nerve had cracked.

He hurried out of the court-room.

Mr Tarpawaller cackled with approval. As I bent to recover a volume of Halsbury from the floor, the words on the open page leapt out at me — 'Never sentence in anger.'

I drank a glass of dusty water.

'You can tell Mr Bhindi he may return to work,' I called to the usher who had retreated to the public gallery.

'You'll have to deal with this mess,' I told Mr Bhindi. 'Meanwhile I shall visit the *locus in quo*.'

The *locus in quo* — Mr Tarpawaller's property — was a narrow whitewashed building adjoining the Gardens of Paradise Bottling Factory. It was let as a boarding-house.

'Judge Overton here,' I called through the latticed portico.

The proprietor appeared. He was wearing an army great-coat, an astrakan hat and an enormous muffler. The shade temperature was 103.

'I have to inspect the premises for the purposes of the Rent Act,' I said.

The proprietor looked mystified, but let me in. He understood no English so I tried to explain the reason for my visit by sign language.

'For me to say,' I demonstrated, 'how much faloos Landlord Tarpawaller take from you.' I had already picked up a smattering of the language. The proprietor exploded into a violent fit of coughing and tightened up his muffler.

'May as well get on with the inspection,' I decided.

The main reception room had a low wooden platform running along both sides.

Six sleeping mats were laid along each platform, providing accommodation for twelve inmates. They were presumably out at work.

I noticed a well outside in the court-yard. Water supply was an important factor in assessing rent.

'Water,' I called to the proprietor. 'Is water good?'

He took no notice. He was crouched over a charcoal brazier, groaning and coughing. The poor man was obviously suffering from 'flu. I had, as always, a bottle of Aspirins in my brief-case, and handed him two. My action was well meaning, but as it turned out, foolish.

In Sheikh Suliman, a European who produced medicaments from a black brief case could only be a doctor. The boarding-house proprietor had assumed I was the new Medical Officer on a routine health call. I suppose I should have realised this, but it never occurred to me at the time.

'Has Mr Tarpawaller given you a rent book?' I persisted, making a scribbling gesture on a memo-pad. 'Paper? Landlord give paper?' I repeated. The proprietor downed his tablets and smiled enigmatically.

'Must remember to check that point with Mr Tarpawaller,' I noted.

From the kitchen, where I examined the rather primitive cooking facilities, a circular stone staircase led upstairs. The upper storey was divided into two.

'Quite understand,' I motioned to the proprietor when we reached a curtained partition on the second floor. 'Purdah quarters beyond here. Wouldn't dream of going in.'

To my surprise, he took me by the arm and insisted upon my entering. He spoke quietly to the veiled lady within.

'Not essential,' I said, making a quick check of the room's dimensions, 'but thank you all the same.'

I was about to go, when to my astonishment the lady began to pull up her dress.

'Good God,' I thought, 'had I blundered into some sort of house of ill fame?'

Her husband, the boarding-house keeper smiled approvingly as she exposed a plump knee for my inspection. She then further startled me by rubbing her hand over her knee and groaning. It was then that I noticed that the limb was swollen. Her husband pointed to the contused joint.

'Him broke?' he demanded.

'Gracious me,' I exclaimed as the truth dawned. Believing that I was the Government doctor on a public health visit, both husband and wife had wished me to examine the lady's injured leg.

Just then I recognised a familiar voice on the terrace beyond the curtains. It was one of the few occasions when I was glad to hear that Mr Bhindi had arrived. Advocate Tarpawaller was with him. I hurriedly joined them.

'Have you gentlemen cleared up your misunderstanding?' I asked. They nodded. 'Then you'd better clear up this one,' I said.

Mr Bhindi proceeded to interpret the true reason for my visit.

Upon learning that she had exposed herself to a Nazarene stranger who was not the Government Doctor at all, the proprietor's wife affected hysteria. Her wailing was taken up by all the other female inhabitants of the purdah quarter.

'For heaven's sake Bhindi,' I urged, 'tell them nobody regrets the mistake more than myself. And they can count upon me for a very fair assessment of rent when I leave.' Mr Tarpawaller beckoned me to a peephole in the verandah parapet. From there I could see that a crowd had gathered below. They were obviously in a very nasty mood.

'Maybe Your Honour vill not be leaving,' he piped.

It seemed that an ugly distortion of the incident had spread around the bazaar.

'Side exit,' signalled Mr Bhindi. He popped a lady's black sheda — purdah-cloak — over my head and led me down some back stairs.

'Where are you taking me?' I whispered, stumbling forward into some sort of carriage, heavy with the scent of jasmine.

'It's the back seat of my motor-car,' hissed Mr Bhindi, 'where I usually hide my wife.' He drew across the dividing curtain and drove me undetected through the hostile throng. To them, at that moment, I was a sex-maddened infidel who had tricked his way into the women's quarters of the boarding house.

'Quick thinking on your part,' I congratulated him when he delivered me safely home. He was about to return to the bazaar to explain to the populace the truth of the situation.

'Perhaps now we hear less from Your Honour about Emancipation of Women,' observed Mr Bhindi.

Chapter Nine

On Probation

'I'm not sure about these Howling Dervishes,' I said to Mr Tarpawaller. 'How far would they respond to probation?'

Mr Tarpawaller's clients, a splinter group of this extreme religious sect, had contravened the Public Order Regulations in Alkazir.

'Vell,' insisted Mr Tarpawaller, 'being first offenders, they all come under the Probation Act.'

As he spoke, the leader of the defendants threw his black cloak down into the well of the court and leapt several feet into the air. 'Yah-hoo,' he called in my direction.

'He is feeling great religious joy,' explained Mr Tarpawaller.

'I'd rather he didn't,' I said. 'This is a court of law, not a mosque.'

'Yahoo,' repeated the leader with another disturbing leap.

'Yah-Hoo is Arabic,' Mr Tarpawaller continued. 'It means 'O Great Power'.'

'Tell him I have no wish to be addressed in that way,' I instructed Mr Tarpawaller.

I turned to the Court Usher. 'See if the learned Clerk has finished his lunch,' I said.

The Probation Officer at Alkazir was Mr Bhindi. It was yet another title he had added to his list of Court Clerk, Official Receiver, Public Trustee, Registrar of Births and Deaths, Commissioner for Oaths, Under-Sheriff, Assistant Master of the Court of Protection and Administrator of Wrecks.

'It seems, Mr Bhindi,' I explained to him when he appeared, 'I've no choice but to place these gentlemen on probation.'

Mr Bhindi reluctantly put away his tooth-pick. 'Up to you,' he said.

He prodded the defendants to their feet with the carved

43

ebony stick he had acquired upon a trading visit to East Africa. As one man, the fanatical pack sprang into the dock. For an instant I feared they were about to break into their infamous 'Whirling Dance'.

'I am placing you on probation,' I announced. 'The court will keep a close check on your progress.'

Mr Bhindi marshalled them away.

From the verandah a kind of banshee howl died away, 'Yahoo, Yahoo, Yahoo . . . . .'

'Mad people is holy,' observed the usher. I tried to imagine our stout padre spinning and howling up the aisle.

'Not in the Anglican community,' I replied.

It was three months later when Mr Bhindi reminded me of certain duties towards the Dervishes.

'You are required to visit their place of abode,' he pointed out. He opened his copy of Hodgkin on Probation of Offenders and shook out the termites. The preface to Hodgkin contained a photograph of a Mr Nelson, the first probation officer in the world, appointed at Bow Street Court in 1876. Mr Nelson wore a frock-coat and a clerical collar. Mr Bhindi studied the photograph carefully.

'Where are the Dervishes living at present?' I inquired.

Mr Bhindi closed the book with a sigh. He hankered after the dignity of Mr Nelson's frock-coat and clerical collar.

'They are camping on the oasis at Malabar,' he told me. Malabar lay in the desert far away from any roads.

'Hardly on the bus route,' I chaffed.

Mr Bhindi polished his spectacles impassively. 'We go there by camel,' he announced.

During the days of preparation that followed I had moments of apprehension. 'True,' I reminded myself, 'my predecessors in medieval times, the assize judges, had travelled the English countryside on horseback.' But my own experience with horses had not given me confidence. Two weeks after I was conscripted, during the war, into the Royal Horse Artillery, my steed had slowed down my army career by throwing me over a gun carriage. 'Camels,' I told myself, 'are more placid than horses.'

Placid was not altogether the word to describe the obstreperous beast chosen by Mr Bhindi for my own particular use.

'Tip top,' Mr Bhindi assured me, 'with strong head-stall on.'

After a brief struggle, my camel was safely harnessed into a squatting position.

'All ready,' said the Court Usher.

The al-shada, or camel saddle, has a front and rear pommel of tamarisk wood. Between the pommels a sheepskin cushion fits snugly over the hump.

'Very comfortable,' I said, once I had my knees into gear on either side. However, one's sense of judicial isolation, as it were, was alarmingly increased when the camel stood up. 'Hold on,' I called, peering down from what by any standard was a dizzy height, 'there must be a camel with shorter legs than this one.'

'Pull the rope to the left of the neck,' said Mr Bhindi. I did so and the camel lurched forward.

'It's no good,' I called, 'there's simply nothing whatsoever to hold on to up here.'

With the aid of several policemen and the court staff I managed to get safely to earth. It was obvious that some alternative must be devised.

'I am having Your Honour's camel fitted with a Dhalla,' Mr Bhindi decided.

The Dhalla turned out to be an elaborate travelling litter made of Berbera sheepskins slung from poles across the camel's back. It had protective screens of basketwork on either side.

'Much more sensible,' I approved, safely installed behind the great winged contraption. Mr Bhindi supervised the attachment of my lead rein to the harness of his own beast.

'Dhalla used only by women and children,' he said as we set off. I could sense his disapproval, even from twenty feet behind him. But at least we were progressing safely and in some dignity.

The loping rhythms of the camel's tread was unexpectedly soothing. It was as though I were being wheeled along in a giant perambulator. I dozed off.

Night was upon us by the time we reached Malabar. A shrouded figure in a white head cloth emerged from under an olive tree.

'Salaam aleikhum,' he greeted me. It was the Dervish

leader. His beard had grown at least six inches and seemed to crackle with a life of its own. He took me by the arm. Goodwill was intended but I couldn't repress an involuntary yelp as his hawk-like talons sank into my elbow. He nodded with a smile and echoed my exclamation.

'He, too, is hungry,' translated Mr Bhindi.

Before the camp fire a frugal supper was laid. Fellow Dervishes exploded from the surrounding tents, each carrying a lighted taper. We all sat down to eat.

'Sorry no meat,' interpreted Mr Bhindi, on behalf of our host. 'The last sheep have strayed into desert and camel too valuable.'

'But this is good,' I demurred, dipping into the bowl of whitish gravy before me. Under Mr Bhindi's scowl I hastily swapped over to my right hand. I never could remember which one was forbidden for eating, by Koranic custom. 'What food is it?'

'Sour camel milk,' explained the Leader. 'It called curds.'

'Ah — curds and whey!' I exclaimed.

The tribal story-teller had been entertaining us with Dervish folk-tales. I felt it was my turn to respond. I was free to do so without making an ass of myself since Mr Bhindi had vanished into the bushes on one of his frequent errands of nature.

'Little Miss Muffet,' I began, seized by the inspiration of the moment, 'Sat on a tuffet, Eating her curds and whey.' In my elation I performed a quick charade, utilizing my travelling camp-stool and one of the milk bowls. 'There came a big spider,' I went on, gathering momentum, 'And sat down beside her, And frightened Miss Muffet away.' At the climacteric moment my start of feigned horror was almost too real. Mr Bhindi had scuttled back out of the shadows and was squatting behind me.

His beady eye swivelled onto me.

'One over the seven, maybe?' he whispered.

'What, on camel's milk?!!' I giggled.

He steadied me as I skidded on a squashed date.

'Dervish curds are always fermented,' he replied. 'Go to head like alcohol.'

I acknowledged the ripple of applause from around the fire as I made my exit. Inside my tent Mr Bhindi tucked my travelling blanket snugly about me. My head was indeed whirling. 'Dam' Dervishes,' I murmured, sinking into oblivion.

The next thing I knew was Mr Bhindi's face at the tent-hole, the sunshine blinding behind him.

'Hanging over, Sir?' he gloated.

'Nothing that a Livingstone Rouser won't put right,' I countered. It was a large pill that only went down when combined with a heavy draught of magnesia. I had learned never to stir from base without my canvas medical holdall — another purchase from the Tropical Outfitters in London.

Mr Bhindi was doubling up as chambermaid this morning. He handed me a bowl of brackish water and supervised my ablutions watchfully. I sometimes felt I was the object of some anthropological study Mr Bhindi was compiling on the Customs and Habits of the British Male in Tropical Conditions.

'These Dervishes,' I began, as I started to shave. I turned away to conceal an unaccountable tick that had developed below my left eye overnight. But the mirror in Mr Bhindi's hand followed me remorselessly.

'Yes, Sir?'

'It's no use pretending that I understand their ecumenical outlook,' I continued. I dipped unobtrusively into the Rousers again. 'But now they've settled quietly on their own out here, they seem to be harming no one.'

'No one?', hinted Mr Bhindi.

'Impartiality is the hallmark of English Justice,' I reminded him. 'I would never allow my personal indisposition or feelings to mar its proper course.'

I threw the soapy water out of the tent, missing Mr Bhindi by a few well-judged inches.

'I have decided to free the Dervishes from all restrictions under the Probation Act,' I told him.

Mr Bhindi, who was still consuming the remains of his breakfast, disposed of a handful of walnut shells into my sandals.

'Your Honour should not do that,' he insisted. 'These men cannot be trusted.'

'Nonsense,' I answered. 'The Probation Order will be discharged in this case when I return to Alkazir.'

47

Further disapproval from Mr Bhindi was cut short by a call from outside. My own breakfast, it seemed, was awaiting me.

'Kindly ensure our camels are harnessed and ready,' I instructed the Clerk.

I followed the Dervish Leader to where my own meal was laid out. A spicy aroma met me from the cooking-pot on the fire. It smelt this time like a non-vegetarian menu.

'For Judge,' said the Dervish Leader.

On to my banana leaf he ladled — clearly in my special honour — a succulent portion of braised liver.

'Return of the lost sheep?!' I exclaimed, tucking in. My host chuckled into his beard. 'A man with a sense of humour,' I approved, 'despite the barriers of creed and custom.'

I had almost finished the dish when Mr Bhindi appeared at my shoulder.

'Our camels ready, Mr Bhindi?' I inquired.

'Mine is,' he replied. He wore a more than usually smug expression.

'And mine?'

Mr Bhindi pointed a finger at the last fragment of meat on my dish.

'Nice and tender?' he inquired.

I nodded, mystified.

'Younger camel make best feast,' declared Mr Bhindi. 'Taken, slaughtered, cooked — while we sleep!'

I listened dumbfounded while Mr Bhindi went on to explain that he had just seen the Dervishes butchering the remainder of my camel behind the encampment.

A Dervish elder interrupted Mr Bhindi's accusations and began an impassioned speech.

'He is saying Your Honour's camel wandered in the night and fell to its death down the ravine.'

'Does he mean that four-foot gully we crossed on our way to the oasis?' I asked.

Mr Bhindi nodded.

'A gross theft of the meanest kind,' I burst out. 'Tell these scoundrels that no one will go unpunished!'

Mr Bhindi drew me to one side. 'Maybe Your Honour is now forgetting Hallmark of English Justice,' he chided. 'Angry suspicion is no proof.'

Our sole remaining means of transport was chewing contentedly in the background. I was scrambling aboard behind Mr Bhindi when he turned towards me.

'Is Your Honour still planning to discharge their Probation Order for good conduct?' he dared to inquire.

The Dervishes parted ranks to let us through. Their leader bowed an impertinent farewell.

'It is reminding me of old Arab proverb,' called Mr Bhindi over his shoulder, as we set off on the return journey to Alkazir.

'The wise man who steals a traveller's beast invites him to the meal.'

Again, I made no reply. Indeed I did not speak to Mr Bhindi for some days afterwards.

Chapter Ten

Tennis with the Sultan

Malakar is a rocky isthmus off the Gulf of Alkazir. It was visited in turn by the Abyssinians, the Malays, the Persians, the Portuguese, the Spanish, the Dutch, the French, the Turks, the Germans, and the British. All were stunned by its repulsive aspect save the British, who built a coaling station there in 1869. The proprietors, Eastern Shipping Ltd of London, had bought the site from Omar IV, Sultan of Alkazir, in return for a large consignment of arms.

In 1934 the coaling station closed down. For twenty years Malakar lay deserted. Then oil was discovered under its crumbling wharves.

'My reward from the Holy Prophet,' claimed the reigning Sultan, Omar V, who had recently endowed a new mosque for the Alkazir sultanate. The local representative for Eastern Shipping Ltd disagreed.

Litigation began in the Supreme Court of British Arabia. The Chief Justice was away on leave and I was taking his place for the first time.

There was another reason for my feeling apprehensive about the occasion. I was not permitted my familiar court setting with its homely, if raucous atmosphere. Under the Judicial Encampment (Mesopotamia, Persian Gulf and Southern Arabia) Regulations (1921), the summer session of the Supreme Court was held in a large Durbar tent. This was fashioned, I was told by Mr Bhindi, who accompanied me, upon the one used by George V, King Emperor, when he received the homage of the Indian Princes at Delhi on 12 December 1911. I was to preside from the central dais, wearing a light wig rather than the Imperial Crown of India.

The weather on the fateful day turned out to be changeable. I was waiting in the wings for a signal from Mr Bhindi, who was laying out the papers on my desk.

'Better slacken off those guy-ropes,' I whispered to him.

The *shamal* — a sudden gust of desert wind — had blown up, causing the marquee to billow and sag. I was reminded of a childhood visit to Bertram Mills' circus when a thunderstorm had broken out. I had always been a timid child and had had to be taken out to be sick.

Fortunately for my nerves on this occasion, the *shamal* died away as quickly as it had come, and danger seemed to have been averted. A faint sigh of disappointment went up from the waiting crowd as I took my place unharmed on the platform. Better things awaited them however. The next moment the entrance flaps to the arena were drawn apart with a flourish. A burly figure, magnificent in black aba and golden burnous, made his appearance, and all heads were bowed.

'His Highness the Sultan of Alkazir,' announced Mr Bhindi.

I beckoned the Sultan forward to a cane chair in the witness stand. His young attendant slipped an embroidered cushion under the ruler's feet. He took the oath with a twinkle in his eye. Several large rings flashed as he settled his robes and smoothed his short black beard.

'My father,' the Sultan began in evidence, speaking perfect English, 'allowed the shipping company to use Malakar for their coaling station. It was a favour, nothing more.'

'But unfortunately, Your Highness,' I pointed out, 'the deed signed by your illustrious ancestor says otherwise.' I extricated the conveyance from the company file.

'It says he was paid for the sale of the land and all that lay beneath it.'

The bland smile remained on the Sultan's plump face. He shook his head quietly.

'His Highness's father,' interjected Mr Bhindi, 'never cut his beard.'

'I don't see what that's got to do with the case,' I rejoined.

Mr Bhindi let forth one of his groans of disapproval at my stupidity.

'In Islam it is a sign of perfect wisdom,' he lectured.

'Would such a great man part with all rights in family land?'

I was studying the conveyance again when there was a disturbance at the back of the court. A group of indigo-painted Bedouin pressed forward, clutching rifles to their naked chests.

'The Sultan's bodyguard,' explained Mr Bhindi. 'They say they must stand between you and His Highness.'

'Certainly,' I agreed, 'provided they surrender their weapons.'

Twenty Mauser rifles clattered on to my desk.

I turned my attention back to the deed of conveyance.

'Your Highness cannot dispute the clear wording and the signature,' I said. I leaned forward and tried to pass over the document but the hand of the Commander of the bodyguard intervened. Eventually the document reached the Sultan.

'Does Your Highness not agree it is your father's signature?' I asked.

The Sultan purported to have forgotten his reading glasses and merely waved it away. The red-turbanned Commander handed it back to me. When I bent to re-examine it, I myself had difficulty in deciphering the vital words. I clicked my tongue irritably. The indigo thumb-marks would undoubtedly cause problems for any court of appeal. It was lucky I had been able to read the document first.

'I'm afraid my ruling must be against Your Highness,' I announced.

The crowd rustled with interest. Someone threw a mangoe at me but it missed.

The Sultan rose and gathered his cloak about him. He seemed to accept the decision without demur. Mr Bhindi, on the other hand, chose this moment to behave with disgraceful partiality.

'Your Honour make bad mistake,' he breathed, behind his hand.

I made a mental note to inquire at the next opportunity as to his business interests in the Sultan's name.

As His Highness swept off, Mr Bhindi led the way out backwards, bending ever lower in the process. He had reckoned, though, without a hole in the matting, and his obsequious charade terminated with an impromptu backwards somersault.

'Mr Bhindi,' I snapped, 'this is not the Big Top. Nor is the British Government paying you for a performance as Coco the Clown.'

Perhaps I should have withheld such a cheap jibe at the expense of someone who, in title at least, was a subordinate. But even the iron control of justice is sometimes known to break. I need not have worried. It was far too esoteric a reference for Mr Bhindi's comprehension.

He returned complacently. 'Karate training,' he announced. 'Come in handy! I teach you sometime.' That was a treat I planned to postpone.

Meanwhile, he sealed my judgement against the Sultan with sulky reluctance, and that concluded my brief session in the Arabian Supreme Court.

However, that was not my final encounter with the losing side in the case.

'Let us try our court this time,' read the message I received, a witty invitation from the Sultan to a game of tennis at his palace. I was on local leave at the time. The up-country Government Rest-House, where I was staying, lay in the hills adjoining his residence.

At the palace, liveried bearers conducted me through the marble colonnades. The Sultan welcomed me with great charm.

'Not too hot for you, Judge Overton?' he inquired.

'So long as Your Highness will permit me to wear this panama I've borrowed from the matron at the Rest-House,' I said. 'She insisted that I bring it along.'

'Headgear essential,' he agreed, producing an old cricket cap, an odd contrast I thought to his flowing robes.

The Sultan took my hand and pointed in the direction of the tennis court. We came to a junction in the path. I was about to lead on through an arched trellis-way covered in jasmine. His Highness's hand on my shoulder brought me back.

'Not that way,' he chuckled. 'I don't imagine the ladies of my household would be quite up to a mixed doubles.'

A tinkle of merry laughter came from the latticework beyond. I was aware of several pairs of hidden eyes following my retreating back.

We took up positions on the sandy court.

'May Allah give thee wings,' announced my opponent from the other end. His remark was addressed, in Arabic, at the tennis ball, which he served at me, underarm and without warning.

'Fifteen points,' claimed the Sultan, adjusting his cricket cap.

I began a protest. There was a warning click from a rifle bolt behind some oleander bushes. I caught a glimpse of a familiar red-turban. It was the Commander of the bodyguard. I lost the game.

We changed ends and my first service began to go in. There was a flurry of sand and His Highness missed a return. It was the first time I had seen him lose his silky composure.

'Burn it into ashes,' he shouted, casting the racquet aside, narrowly missing his private secretary, a scholarly-looking man in spectacles, who was watching anxiously on the side line. Two ball-boys scurried forward laden with new racquets.

The Sultan's next drive hit the top of the net and fell back. To my astonishment, he drew a gold jambia from his waist and struck at the net. 'I have destroyed an evil jin,' he explained, with a wry smile.

We were soon hard at it again, 'Like the sun,' quipped the Sultan, 'there is much fire in me.' A long rally followed which His Highness won.

The senior ball-boy took advantage of the interval when we changed ends to sprinkle his master with rose-water, while I was offered a glass of lime. The Sultan made a careful examination of his side of the court. A tiny furrow was detected. He summoned another minion and a small donkey was led out with a log roller to put this right.

Revived again, His Highness ordered play to recommence. Pounding heavily to and fro he made a close game of it. Eventually I neared match point.

'Stop,' requested the Sultan, dropping his racquet and turning towards Mecca. High up in a minaret of the palace mosque, the holy man was calling the faithful to prayer. This time a procession of retainers filed on to the court bearing hand-bowls, towels, and prayer mats.

'Now,' said His Highness, rising in due course from his

devotions, 'I feel the strength of twenty Bedouin.' Like a Wimbledon champion he began smashing balls away. I started to lose points. 'Ah,' he called, 'the victory is slipping through your fingers like sand.' Unnerved, I surrendered the match.

We rested upon a pile of carpets on the verandah where the air was rich with incense.

'So much depends,' beamed the Sultan, handing me a choice segment of water melon, 'upon one's choice of courts.'

Regrettably I did not get the chance of a return match. A few months later I was posted to the South Seas.

Chapter Eleven

Trial by Jury in the South Seas

The first of my predecessors as British Judge in the South
Seas, was the famous Knight of the Sandwich Isles, Charles
St. Stephen, (1810-1882). His legal career had started in
Sydney, where he was the Law Reporter. A wanderer by
temperament, St. Stephen was soon travelling in Oceania.
Succumbing to the spell of Robert Louis Stevenson's Golden
Isles, he became Hawaiian Chargé d'Affaires for Southern
Polynesia. In reward for his services in this exotic post, he
was knighted by the Sovereign of the Sandwich Isles.

His last post in the South Pacific was in Lovaka. There he
became Lord Chief Justice to Tombi, the Cannibal King of
Bua.

The first case heard by Sir Charles, in his midget court-
house on the hillside of King Tombi's capital, Lovaka,
reflected the bizarre disorder of that beachcombing community. It concerned a Filipino known as Looey, the cook on
a labour schooner. Looey had killed a fellow sailor with a
knife. Sir Charles condemned him to death and he was to be
hanged on the morning of 27 May 1872. All preparations for
the execution had been completed, but the hangman had
failed to appear because of his wife's illness. The execution
had therefore been postponed. Looey's lawyer at once
petitioned the Chief Justice to secure the condemned man's
release on the ground that the sentence had not been carried
out as directed. Sir Charles dismissed the application. He
ordered the hanging to take place next morning. At 7 am on
29 May, Looey was again placed over the trap. However, the
rope, left in position overnight, had become swollen by the
rain and would not run in the noose. When the hangman
pulled the bolt, the noose caught upon Looey's chin. Stunned
by the drop, Looey hung for about ten minutes. Then he

began to struggle, calling to the bystanders to shoot him and end his misery. The only solution was to cut the rope. Looey was returned to his cell while King Tombi and Sir Charles were consulted. The King granted a reprieve, but for Sir Charles, the 'Looey case' was not over. In preparation for his execution, Looey had made a will directing how his savings were to be distributed. He returned from the scaffold to find his directions already carried out. His money had been spent upon a merry rum-party by his grief-stricken friends. Sir Charles resolved the problem by arranging compensation for Looey out of public funds. Looey remained in the Lovaka jail for some years and was then deported.

During 1873, various up-country tribes rebelled against King Tombi. Learning that several hundred insurrectionists had been captured, Sir Charles advised the King to indict them for high treason. I studied the case records left by Sir Charles. His notes of evidence were pencilled in a shaky hand. Court sittings were short, with frequent adjournments to one or other of the fifty-two public houses in the settlement. Applying the principle that everyone that appeared before him was either guilty or a fool, Sir Charles convicted everybody. He awarded long terms of imprisonment in all cases, but the prisoners served their sentences in an unusual way. They were hired out by the King to work for European planters in Vola Seru, the main island of the group.

At times, Sir Charles sat with an assistant judge, an island noble unversed in the law, who had great difficulty in understanding the English language. For this problem the Lord Chief Justice had an immediate solution. The only way to make a foreigner understand English was to shout at him. Thus, instead of discreetly whispering the instructive passage in his volume of English Criminal Law to his brother judge on the bench, Sir Charles would bellow the whole chapter into the poor man's ear — much to the irritation of anglers in the river nearby.

Sir Charles favoured jury trial in the Bua Islands. In Lovaka, he obtained the assistance of European jurors, some of whom were peculiarly well versed in court procedure. These were the escaped convicts from Australia, who had acquired their knowledge in the dock at the Old Bailey.

Outside the capital, jurymen were less easily recruited. Sir Charles used to tell a story of a visit he made to an outlying island.

The Chief Justice had reached a remote village in the middle of the island. There he planned to hold court. The village chief had one prisoner awaiting trial — upon a charge of murder.

'We must first empanel a jury,' directed Sir Charles from his barkcloth litter under the coconut trees. His interpreter explained to the villagers what was required. 'Swear in the twelve good men and true,' the judge proceeded. After hearing the evidence, Sir Charles summed up to the jury. 'Consider your verdict, gentlemen,' he concluded. The jurors retired to a nearby thicket.

Sir Charles was preparing for a paddle in the lagoon when his interpreter rushed up to him. 'Come quickly, Lordship,' he urged, 'there is great trouble.' Easing on his mosquito boots, Sir Charles answered the call of duty.

It seemed that fighting had broken out among the jurors. By the time he had reached the fracas, four of the jurymen were unconscious, the rest stood around in hang-dog silence. All bore marks of violence. 'Am I to assume, gentlemen,' Sir Charles inquired, 'that you are not agreed upon your verdict?' There was no reply.

'Bear in mind,' he went on, 'the jury must fast until a verdict is reached. Neither fire, food nor candle, as the English Common Law has it.'

Sir Charles withdrew to his *lakalumoa*, the palm-leaf canopy customarily erected by the Buans for visitors of importance. The long sticky afternoon drew to a close. At dusk the air became cooler, and Sir Charles, exhausted by his long journey, fell asleep. When he opened his eyes again it was already sunrise.

'We shall resume court at once,' he told the interpreter. He returned to the coconut grove — 'Mother Nature's Old Bailey', as Sir Charles referred to it.

'Where's the prisoner?' he demanded, the jury having appeared.

'It was a long hungry night for them, Lordship,' stammered the interpreter, indicating the jurors as they filed into their bamboo box. 'Cannibal customs die hard in these islands.'

60

'Poor wretch,' Sir Charles would conclude, when recounting the tale to his paling dinner guests, 'he was simply the victim of a unanimous verdict.'

Fortunately, well before my own arrival in the South Pacific, juries were fed at Government expense. However, the islands had other surprises in store for me, including gastronomical ones.

Chapter Twelve

Customs of the Country

'Baked yowl, fried in gung,' said His Excellency. 'I trust you like our native food?'

'Oh yes, sir,' I growled, my teeth locked in the gung. As visiting Assize Judge in the British South Pacific territories, I was a guest at Government House on the principal island. 'Can't understand people working out here who eat only English dishes,' he snapped, 'when there are so many native delicacies to hand.'

A sauce bowl was lowered past my ear.

'Don't be afraid of it,' called H.E., as the bearer swamped my plate in green foam. 'It's an island relish, very palatable.'

There was a rattling at my side. It came from the throat of a fellow guest who had just tasted the relish. Kindly servants soon helped him from the table.

I bit savagely into a slice of yowl.

'Your trials all going smoothly this trip?' inquired the island Commissioner of Police.

'Up until now,' I replied through my tears.

'Try the salad,' cried the Governor.

'Tropical nettles,' warned the Police Chief, too late.

'English wives with their baked custards, they lost us India,' declared His Excellency. 'There's no colour bar where we all eat the same food.'

The Governor signalled and six servants filed out onto the lawn. They carried trowels. 'Just digging out the earth ovens,' he explained. The servants began work, engulfed in flame. Smoke filled the dining-room. 'Excellent,' approved the Governor, 'the meat will be well done.'

'So delightfully British,' remarked the American wife of an Anglican bishop. The bishop choked discreetly into his handkerchief. 'I just loved that yowl,' said his wife through the haze.

Outside, excavations were proceeding briskly. The six bearers padded back inside. They carried a tureen emblazoned with the royal coat-of-arms. There was a flash as the Governor uncovered the tureen. He beamed over the molten black flesh. 'Now, you roll the meat into a ball with the thumb and forefinger thus,' he demonstrated. We rolled our meat balls on the Wedgwood dinner service.

'There's jolly well no lack of vitamins in this, sir,' said a visiting anthropologist, between spasms.

'That's why the people in these parts are so robust,' replied His Excellency.

The native band on the terrace was playing selections from *Oklahoma*.

'Ever see the show?' asked the Governor's ADC.

'No,' I muttered, slipping another lump of yowl upon the ledge under the table.

'Have a glass of root cup,' said His Excellency.

'I'll stick to the solids if you don't mind, sir,' I demurred, stabbing another forkfull of grey sludge. 'I suppose one gets to like these exotic dishes,' I murmured to my neighbour, the District Officer.

'Never,' he sighed, in silent mastication, 'but I don't want to lose my job.'

'A remarkable fruit,' proclaimed the Governor, as we began the dessert. 'Just eat the pips, leave the reat,' he warned, 'it's poisonous. You'll find the pips simply delicious, but do first scrape them clean.'

We got through the fruit with only one casualty, a bearded Sikh at the end of the table, who proved a careless scraper.

'Ladies and Gentlemen, the Sovereign,' boomed the Governor, above the sound of my hiccups. He took me by surprise. I was hunched over my finger-bowl, drinking water from the wrong side.

'Such a cute way to drink the loyal toast,' cried the bishop's wife admiringly.

The ladies hurried away.

'Gather round, gentlemen,' commanded the Governor. We formed a flatulent circle about him. 'Did you know the islanders smoke their own version of the hookah?' he said with pride. His Excellency indicated a pile of bladders and bamboo-piping at his feet. The bladders gurgled sullenly.

'Don't inhale too much,' he cautioned, passing the mouth-piece to the bishop.

'Very fragrant,' gasped the bishop, ashen faced.

A village choir began to sing for us under the candelabra.

The Governor unstoppered a decanter. 'Try our mangrove liqueur,' he urged, savouring the bouquet. 'They brew it in the swamp, you know.' We held back appalled by its malicious orange colour. The Governor drank steadily. At last he spoke. 'Shall we join the ladies?' he said.

We helped each other on to the terrace. I searched Government House for an empty bathroom but all nine were occupied. When I returned the stronger guests had begun to leave. The Governor shook my hand. 'Just a minute, Judge,' he said, while a bearer stowed a covered basket in the boot of my car.

'H.E. never sends a guest away without a little gift,' whispered the ADC.

'What's in it?' I asked, deeply touched.

'Only two dozen yowl and a bag of gung,' smiled the ADC as I ricocheted away.

Next morning my court clerk kindly relieved me of the yowl. He parcelled it out to thirty-four of his wife's relations. The gung he kept for himself.

Somehow, the South Sea Islands seemed to affect their British Administrators with a burning passion to adopt local custom. And not merely in matters of food. Sir Edward Warburton had antimacassars of bark-cloth affixed to every Waring and Gillow chair of the State Drawing Room. In the principal Guest Suite, Sir Howard Bartle substituted log-shaped wooden headrests for pillows — the kind favoured by the Melanesian Bigheads to preserve their elaborate hair styles. The boom of hide-war drums summoned guests to breakfast under the regime of Sir Rigby and Lady Saunders. Sir Hugh Wyn-Roberts became an adept on the Tongan nose flute, much to the dismay of his captive audience at Vice Regal musical evenings.

Sir Arthur Gordon, an early Governor of the Western Pacific, always trod the islands bare-foot, in native fashion. His officials were requested to do the same. However, his fondness for the island way of life firmly excluded one particular Polynesian practice. This was the softening up of

65

those in authority with the tactful presentation of gifts whenever necessary. On the contrary, Sir Arthur had the law tightened up in such matters. Even minor cases of official corruption were prosecuted with the utmost severity under his eagle eye. I had often perused his edicts on the subject, preserved in mildewed clothboard at the Government Archives. I had them much in mind on that particular Assize, since there was a long corruption case for trial.

Mr Manikswol, the auditor, was charged with numerous counts of fraudulent conversion. Having ample funds at his disposal, he had booked out the only hotel in the settlement, a whitewashed building like a Wild West saloon. I was obliged to move out to a small annexe at the rear. Unfortunately, we still had to share the same bathroom.

'Better be first in,' I decided, setting my alarm an hour earlier for the next day.

Dawn was breaking as I tiptoed past Mr Manikswol's bedroom door. His heavy snoring muffled my usual struggle with the kerosene water-heater. It had to be a nifty tub because of leakage through a faulty plug fitting.

I was still sitting in two or three inches of tepid water when I suddenly realised that I was no longer alone. The snoring had ceased and somebody was gargling on the other side of the bamboo screen between bath and basin.

'Bathroom's engaged,' I called.

The suave face of Mr Manikswol, draped in the bathroom's only towel, appeared above the screen.

'Room for two, eh Judge?' he sallied.

There was no reply to brashness of this sort.

Clothing myself in a tablet of medicated soap, I snatched up my pyjamas and withdrew.

The following morning I tried to reverse the batting order. For well over an hour I endured the cacophony of plungings, wallowings and other unimaginable bathroom athletics.

'All yours, Judge,' shouted the indefatigable Manikswol, leaving an odious trail of puddles down the passageway. It was in fact the only trace of water left. An overhead clanking from the cistern and a smell of singeing in the heating apparatus told me there would be no bath for me that day. The bathroom, I decided reluctantly, would have to be avoided for the time being.

A body sponge was a poor substitute for a dip, in the heat of the tropics. The case dragged on for five sticky days. On the sixth morning, when my need was becoming desperate, the jury obligingly convicted. The bathroom was at last free — unlike, I regret to say, Mr Manikswol.

One last case remained in my list. A youth called Rami, the tearaway son of a local sugar-cane farmer, was indicted for maliciously wounding a neighbour. It was the climax of a long-standing feud over land.

When I was leaving my hotel for court to hear this case, an envelope bearing the Government House crest was handed to me.

'Well that settles it,' I told the Clerk, as I took my seat on the Bench. I had just opened the missive from Government House. It was an invitation to dinner again that night.

'We must finish this case today,' I announced.

'But the defence is calling twelve witnesses,' he pointed out. This was true. They were strewn across the court steps fast asleep.

'Then the sooner we get started, the better,' I replied.

There was a ship leaving at dusk. With a bit of luck I could be on board by then, leaving behind a polite note to the Governor saying I was urgently required at my next port of call.

'Anything,' I decided, 'to avoid another night of disaster at His Excellency's dinner table.'

The hot morning wore on. The prosecution closed its case.

'Your turn now, Rami,' I said to the accused.

Rami, the Marlon Brando of the cane fields, wore a leather jacket and jeans. He opened his defence in a sort of Transatlantic accent, learned at the island cinema.

'Gen-l-men of the jury,' he drawled, 'I got myself an alibi. Guess where I was at the time this crime was committed?' The jury perked up. 'I was speedin' along the beach on a motorbike with my girlfriend on the back.'

The girlfriend, Rami's star witness, turned out to be a lady of generous proportions. She was equally generous with the truth. After cross-examination by the prosecution, she was obliged to admit with a smile that her story supporting Rami's alibi must be false.

'So everything you said was untrue?' I interjected.

'Not everything,' she answered happily, 'I give my true name.'

The girlfriend was followed into the witness-box by the eleven other defence witnesses, all relatives of the prisoner. I was somewhat pre-occupied during the next hour recording their perjured evidence in longhand. It was the wheezing of witness number nine, the prisoner's cousin, which prompted me to look up. To my surprise the court-room was full of smoke. What plot was this? I wondered. A ruse to set the prisoner free? Or was the rival faction in the case taking the law into its own hands and planning to incinerate the prisoner, along with the Judge?

'Just the last stage in the cane-cutting process,' explained the Clerk. Apparently, the farmer in the field adjoining the court-house was burning the stubble after harvesting the sugar-cane.

'If Your Honour would care to adjourn,' he suggested, 'it will be all clear by tomorrow.'

'I can't do that,' I announced. The prospect of another evening with yowl and gung at Government House drove me on.

At long last the time arrived for me to sum up to the jury.

'Gentlemen,' I addressed them, raising my voice above the crackling of the fire, 'can you all hear me?'

'We can hear you, my lord,' called back the foreman, 'but we can't quite see you.' Dusk was falling and the smoke in the court-room had rendered it very dim.

'You can take it I am still here,' I was able to reassure them.

The jury retired for less than five minutes.

'Unanimous verdict of guilty,' announced their foreman, his head silhouetted against a skyline blackened with smoke.

Rami accepted his sentence in good part.

'Justice done there all right,' said the Clerk as I stepped out of court.

'If not quite seen to be done,' was my obvious reply.

I was still coughing slightly as we made our way past the smouldering cane field en route for the boat.

'Smoke no good for throat,' sympathised the Clerk.

'Better than His Excellency's mangrove liqueur,' I decided.

68

Chapter Thirteen

A Break in the Circuit

'Can't beat your full-bottomed wig for dignity,' called JS from the front of our launch.

'Feels a bit out of place at the moment,' I said, lunging into the scuppers after one of my buckle shoes.

JS was a Resident Commissioner of some fame on the outer fringes of my judicial parish. Although he himself presented an informal appearance — a tall disjointed figure with a wild thatch of hair, in a tattered golfing blazer over army trousers, he had insisted that as visiting judge I should actually come ashore in red robes and wig.

'It impresses the islanders with the majesty of English law,' he urged.

My grey horsehair curls were flapping primly in the trade wind.

'Lucky they've never heard of Father Christmas out here,' I quipped, 'they might mistake me for his mother.'

The police band, resplendent in their red and white uniforms, was lined up on the jetty. As we landed the buglers sounded a fanfare.

'Arranged for your arrival to coincide with our evening flag-lowering ceremony,' JS explained. The drummers began to beat the retreat.

'Follow me to the dais,' whispered JS, indicating a raised wooden platform beside the flag-pole.

I would have been up there in a jiffy if my judge's knee-breeches had not been braced up to my armpits. Complete with heavy garters they had me gripped like plaster casts.

'Either get on or off,' said JS, 'the flag's half-way down already.'

I had in fact no time to do either. With a clash of cymbals the band broke into the national anthem and I was obliged to make my bow in a somewhat unconventional attitude.

'Don't worry,' said JS, 'they wouldn't know what to expect from Father Christmas or his mother.'

Two grinning bandsmen stepped forward upon JS's command. 'At the double now, lads,' he told them. They picked up my law books and other belongings and set off towards an open two-seater parked under the coconut trees.

'I boast the only motor in the islands,' JS informed me. It was an early French model painted in green stripes. 'Specially camouflaged for bird-watching,' he claimed. JS folded himself into the front seat. 'Put the Judge in the dicky,' he instructed the bandsmen.

JS let out the clutch with a jerk and reversed at high speed along the precipitous coastal track. It struck me as dangerous, but JS seemed to know most of the twists in the road. At each corner JS blew upon a hunting horn.

'Will it only go backwards?' I inquired after a while. Even on trains, travelling backwards has an unsettling effect on me. 'Do we have to make the whole journey like this?'

'No, no,' JS reassured me, 'just for a few miles. It's the only way to loosen up the mesh so that I can use the front gears.'

We stopped at a village where we were presented with tropical fruit and a sucking pig.

'Afraid you'll have to make room for it with you,' said JS. I spent the rest of the journey peering anxiously through a grille of bananas with a porker under my scarlet tippet.

Eventually we came to a halt outside a large wooden house overlooking the bay. 'The Residency,' said JS. 'Your room is at the side.' My guest suite contained no sign of a bed.

'Don't approve of beds,' JS told me, 'most unhealthy. Got rid of them all when Edith went back.' Rumour had it that JS's wife had been on long leave since 1922.

Bed or no bed, it was a great relief to be safely indoors and to get out of my hot robes at last. 'Good chance to freshen up,' I decided, making for the ablutions.

'Use the tub at my end,' called JS, just in time.

One doesn't expect to find a young crocodile in the guest-room bath, even though one's host is a keen naturalist.

I rescued my towel and retreated.

'Feeling all right, old chap?' demanded JS as I faltered past.

'Oh yes,' I insisted, 'quite a break in the usual circuit routine, though.'

After supper JS played his gramophone, the earliest model I had ever seen. He had four badly cracked records, all operatic. The first side he tried was unplayable. He turned the record over. 'Now for a bit of *Tosca*,' he announced. I sat politely through 'Elucevan le stelle', the performance of which was lavishly extended whenever the needle stuck.

'I see I'm trying your local witch doctor tomorrow,' I remarked. I was endeavouring to read the case papers in preparation for the next day.

'What for?' asked JS, winding away at the gramophone.

'Failing to make rain,' I answered. For once my host was nonplussed.

'Hardly a crime,' he countered.

'It is if you take money from the villagers that way,' I explained. 'Obtaining by false pretences, contrary to the Larceny Act.'

As I spoke there came a flash of lightning beyond the verandah and then thunder and lightning. 'Sultry weather,' I said. A cloud burst almost drowned my comment.

'There goes your case,' laughed JS in triumph, as the rain pelted down. 'Some witch doctor, eh? We reckon him the best there is in these parts!'

I pointed out that there were many other counts in the indictment preferred against the wily magician, but JS was no longer interested. He gave an enormous yawn and stretched to his full six and a half feet. He picked up a pile of barkcloth and threw it over my arm. 'Time to turn in,' he boomed. 'You'll get a far better night's sleep on this than on any of your damned Slumberlands.'

The storm was still raging as I prepared for rest. Once again my set of the *Laws of England* proved invaluable. Neatly stacked around my head they made an excellent shield against the appalling draughts that whipped through every crevice in the room. The next day dawned fine and sunny.

'Breakfast,' came the roaring summons from the verandah. I arrived to find my host in an unconventional position.

'Always eat lying on the left side,' he said from the low

72

charpoy alongside the table. 'Gets the juices racing downhill from the pancreas into the duodenum.'

He was busy dipping bread and butter soldiers into his sixth boiled egg.

'I suppose you'll be expecting a Bench to sit on, Judge!' He slapped his thigh and laughed uproariously at his joke, but at that moment a tiny old native appeared, dragging a canvas chair.

'Good boy, Narle,' approved my host. 'Always keep a chair about the place,' JS explained. 'For self-defence.' It was certainly not kept for comfort, I discovered. 'Yes, indeed,' JS continued, 'when taken unawares and unarmed, one can always present the chair. The legs are very confusing to an enraged fanatic.'

In some ways I would have preferred to be confronted by the fanatic rather than the huge bowl of porridge which lay in wait for me at the table. It was topped by a mound of grated coconut.

'An unusual combination,' I suggested, trenching out the nearest corner with my spoon.

JS did not hear me. He had sprung up and was seated at what looked like a harmonium at the far corner of the verandah.

'Came out with the missionaries fifty years ago — still good as new,' said JS. 'Always limber up for the day at the keyboard. How about 'Dreamy Days on the Lagoon'?' He crashed down into a sequence of violent and unrelated chords.

'Don't think I know it,' I called.

'You wouldn't, it's one of mine,' he retorted.

The top of the harmonium was covered with an interesting gallery of shrunken heads and faded photographs.

'Relatives of yours?' I asked.

'Just the pictures,' he replied.

He switched abruptly from symphonic to vamp. Sepia ancestors in Victorian plumes and helmets shimmied along the polished surface to the beat of 'Black Bottom'. JS proceeded to list them from left to right.

'Great Uncle Rufus — Skinner's Horse — lost both ears to a sepoy in The Mutiny — devil's own luck though — lived to go down on the poop of a sloop in the Bay of Bengal.'

He pulled out the Vox Humana stop and launched into 'Rose Marie I Love You'.

'That one's Great Grandfather Haze — commanded a Maori tribe of Royalists — "We always fight naked," the Chief told him — "Mind if I come in my dressing gown?" was grandfather's reply.'

I peered over his shoulder.

'And who's that?' I said, pointing to a bewhiskered gentleman bulging out of his bush jacket and leopardskin cummerbund.

'His fame was confined to the billiards room at the Planters Club,' said JS. 'Only man who could get round all four walls without touching the floor. The Human Fly of Fatibahore they called him. Won a fortune in bets.'

Narle was now pointedly flicking down the breakfast table with a bundle of dried leaves.

'Office time, sahib,' he interrupted, pointing to a large Micky Mouse clock on the sideboard.

'Great Scott, yes,' said JS. He bounded up to the Marconi transmitter which stood under his tank of tropical fish, and twirled the knobs.

The familiar chimes from London boomed out the hour — twelve hours behind ours.

Narle paused reverently in his dusting.

'Big Benny,' he breathed.

'He insists it's the voice of some damned god,' said JS.

JS picked up a battered Gladstone bag and led the way to the car. He was off for the week on safari to the interior of the island. Narle scampered after us, half buried in a mountain of mosquito netting.

'Make sure you tuck it well in,' directed JS, as the helpful midget fixed the gauzey canopy over the top of the motor.

'The mosquitoes can be malarial where I'm going,' explained JS, 'so I like to play it safe.'

It took Narle some minutes to drape the vehicle to his master's satisfaction, but at least this time there was no trouble with the gear box, and we set off normally enough. Although from my place in the dickey, the view through the mesh was necessarily hazy.

As we approached a village, old men and children ran for shelter at the sight of the phantom vehicle bearing down on them out of the forest.

'You'd think they'd be used to it by now,' complained JS, 'it must be the sight of a stranger.'

He flashed an irritable look at me over his shoulder.

'What on earth are you doing up there?' he demanded.

'The only way to get my robe box in the dickey was to sit on it,' I replied.

'Well, at least you could put your umbrella down,' he expostulated. 'After last night's downpour we won't get rain again for weeks.'

It seemed neither the time nor the place to explain my old problem with sunburn, which was one of my continual crosses in the tropics. Anyway, we had arrived at the Court House.

'Do try to cut out the eccentricities, old boy,' said JS, clamping my shoulder in a fatherly fashion. 'The white man on his own has to be a bit of a conformist or he goes all to pot.'

He nipped back under his white canopy.

'Best of luck with them,' he called. 'Until we meet again.' With a farewell toot of the hunting horn, he floated off into the distance like the bridal procession from *Lohengrin*.

After JS's departure I continued to billet at his house until the session was concluded. Narle did his best to brighten up my evenings by producing a black and gold tin of Harrogate Toffees after dinner.

'Master's Lollies,' he would explain, rationing me to a selection of two on each occasion.

My work at court, which ended that particular visit, concerned a boring dispute over pasturing rights. All in all it was a total anticlimax after my extraordinary introduction to island life à la JS.

Looking back to those years, I find it difficult now to believe that such characters as JS ever existed. But he was only one of several. Years of service in torrid climates, accentuated by isolation from conventional society may be some sort of explanation. There was Hamish McKenzie, for example, JS's counterpart, years earlier, on Funafola.

'Unconvincing farce,' I decided, when reconstructing the strange finale in McKenzie's own career.

All Resident Commissioners in the area were empowered to make local bye-laws under various Statutes, in matters of

Health, Public Works, Development, and so on. It was part of the job of the visiting judge to check upon such regulations. Occasionally the Judge might have to declare bye-laws or regulations *ultra vires* as lawyers say. To pronounce, in other words, that the Commissioner had exceeded his powers, 'an excess of jurisdiction' in legal language.

JS, I was to learn upon subsequent visits, had made some pretty odd regulations. Nothing, however, compared with what one of my early predecessors, Mr Justice Baldwin, had encountered when he visited Funafola, in Hamish McKenzie's time, just before the First World War.

Chapter 14

An Excess of Jurisdiction

To Hamish McKenzie, a Fifeshire man, slumber had never been more sweet that toil. He did not approve of any land, even a remote South Seas atoll, in which it always seemed afternoon. Why, I wondered, was he appointed Resident Commissioner, Funafala? It was only when writing this book that I came to know the answer, which I must keep for a later chapter.

Robert Louis Stevenson thought Funafala the most beautiful of the coral islands. 'Nights of a heavenly brightness,' he wrote, 'and the clash of the surf on the reef.' The men of the island could spear fish, climb palm trees, grow taro, make bonito hooks and catch fish. If they felt like it. They rarely did. Hamish McKenzie, on the other hand, was a man who snapped out of bed at dawn. He liked to put in three hours' work before breakfast. He was the only European on the island, but far too busy to notice any lack of companionship.

Within two months of his arrival, the new Commissioner had filled his tiny thatched office on the headland with draft bye-laws. 'Development Regulations', he termed them. His bulky files embraced in earnest detail such subjects as Fishing Grounds, Timber Cutting, Mining Prospects, Land Conservation, Co-operative Farming, Insect Pest Clearance and the Destruction of Noxious Weeds. Occasionally he took time off to lecture the villagers.

'You can't just lie about waiting for the coconuts to fall,' he remonstrated.

'But we don't,' replied the Funafalans politely. 'That is the duty of our womenfolk.'

The Resident Commissioner threw up his fists in despair. 'A murrain on your womenfolk too,' he fulminated. 'They could well set you a better example.' Regrettably the women

of Funafala were renowned not for their industry but for their looks. They spent their time picking up nuts, combing their hair and making love whenever possible, which was always.

Some weeks after his arrival the new Commissioner was working late at his Development plans, wrapped in a heavy plaid dressing-gown, when a sudden wind blew out the oil lamp. 'Drat,' he exclaimed, springing up to relight it — a task which was never effected. The next moment the lamp itself had crashed to the ground and the sudden wind was a howling gale. The privilege of living on the most elevated site on the island had its snags, especially during the hurricane season.

By the time the cyclone had passed over, Hamish McKenzie was without a house. His office, too, had gone. Apart from a few books, he had lost all his draft Development Bye-Laws. This was bad enough. What was far, far worse in his opinion was that he could not replace them. The storm had destroyed every scrap of paper he possessed, along with his writing equipment. It would be two years before the Royal Naval Squadron from Singapore would again visit the island with fresh supplies. 'No Development work for the whole of my tour of office,' he groaned.

For three days he paced desperately up and down the white sands. He could think of nothing to do. On the afternoon of the fourth day he was obsessively clipping his oleander bushes into neat ornamental shapes with a surviving pair of office scissors, when inspiration came. 'What was the Funafalan's only fault?' he asked himself. The answer was simple. Indolence. It was in their blood. He dropped the scissors with a start. He couldn't think why he hadn't grasped the solution before. The obvious plan was to cross the Funafalans with a race well known for its industry. Hamish McKenzie strode down to the beach, removed his kilt and plunged into the lagoon. Surfacing at the reef he stood shaking the water off his tall white frame. He was built like a Lanark pine. 'McKenzie,' he addressed himself sternly, 'your duty's clear.'

I have mentioned at the end of the last chapter my own astonished reaction to the Hamish McKenzie saga. Total disbelief must have registered with my predecessor Mr

Justice Baldwin. It was during his Michaelmas circuit of 1912 that he paid an unsolicited call on Hamish McKenzie in Funafala. There, over a bottle of gin, the Commissioner recounted to the bewildered judge how he had set out 'to beget with child' as he phrased it, the entire female population of the island.

'Drunken ramblings', was of course the judge's first assumption. Gradually, however, as the incredible details were confirmed, it became apparent that the Commissioner was telling no less than the truth.

The Population Development Regulation, Schedule A, was the master-file number given by Hamish McKenzie to his extraordinary undertaking. To this project he had solemnly dedicated himself — 'without fear or favour, prejudice or ill will' as he noted in his files, recalling the oath he had sworn upon assuming office.

Before his promotion to Funafala, McKenzie's service, as I was to discover, had been in a less exotic post. Thus, to familiarise himself with the anthropological background of his new station, he had apparently spent much of his leave in the archives of the Polynesian Society. There he had learned that in such a South Seas island community the voice of the tribal chiefs is paramount.

For Schedule A, therefore, he knew from the outset that he must first obtain the approval of the Funafalan elders. 'I should like to call a meeting,' he had explained to them. The old men listened attentively while the Resident Commissioner pointed out the unique advantages of Fifeshire stock. Schedule A was surprisingly well received. Apart from certain ladies, exempt by marriage or age, the Chiefs had no objection. 'But did the Commissioner appreciate,' they inquired delicately, 'that there were nearly 70 eligible partners? No doubt the men of Scotland were of god-like strength, nevertheless. . . .'

'First things first, gentlemen,' demurred the Commissioner gruffly. 'We shall get down to detailed regulations later.'

He had already mapped out an agenda on the sand. 'Stage One' he had written, with a pointed guava stick — 'Legislation'. 'Stage Two — Organization'. 'Stage Three — Implementation'.

News of the proposed Schedule A soon spread among the

excited ladies of the island. Some of the more forward of them began to leave garlands of hibiscus flowers in the Commissioner's bure. These were not acknowledged. The Resident Commissioner was entirely preoccupied with Stage Two of the Schedule. His future offspring, he had decided, must be suitably educated. He claimed to have conducted classes, through a bemused interpreter, in porridge and haggis making. He certainly gave lessons on Scottish history, for this is recorded in his files. 'William Wallace', we can picture him explaining to his simpering class, 'was a great Scottish leader. He defeated the English at Stirling Bridge in 1297.' No doubt the girls tittered uncomprehendingly. 'Robert Bruce,' the lesson must have proceeded, 'won another great victory for Scotland at Bannockburn in 1314.' Meanwhile his audience would whisper together in the Funafalan dialect, a mixture of Gilbertese and Samoan. Apparently there was only one point of Scottish tradition in which they were interested. 'Beneath his fine red and green skirt, was Mista McKenzie clothed or unclothed?' There are some questions asked the world over.

Although a staunch Presbyterian, Hamish McKenzie had no misgivings over the morality of the Plan. He was well versed in the Scriptures. Jacob, like himself, had dwelt in a strange land — the land of Canaan. The Lord had said unto Jacob, 'Be fruitful and multiply' — Genesis 35, Verse 11. Jacob, he recalled, had acted upon this advice with a surprising number of handmaidens — hence the Twelve Tribes of Israel.

Like all British Administrators, Hamish McKenzie still considered himself bound by English Statutes to follow native tradition in all domestic matters. 'On Funafala,' the elders told him, 'everything rests with the Moon.' They explained what they meant in rather intimate detail. They even prepared a Lunar Calendar in the centre of the village. Each of the girls was given a number and a date in the Lunar Calendar. 'Mista McKenzie,' they apologised, 'would be great busy man.'

Stage Three of the Schedule was to begin at the first quartering of the October moon. At this juncture Hamish McKenzie could no longer afford to ignore the offerings of hibiscus flowers. The largest bunches came from Matilda, daughter of the leading Chief, who had persistently scratched at his sleeping mat each night. She was determined to have pride of place among the Commissioner's brides. 'So be it,' decreed the elders. Preparations were at once set in hand for the Commissioner's first Schedule A Honeymoon. 'Have I forgotten anything?' pondered the Commissioner, his mind a vast compendium of draft regulations through which he was constantly re-checking. 'No,' he concluded, 'I think not. All that remains is the, er, implementation.'

This was probably the first time in his life that Hamish McKenzie had caught himself faltering. The reason, as my predecessor gruffly pointed out, can easily be guessed. So far as the ladies were concerned, Commissioner McKenzie was no man of the world. True, he had once gone beagling alone with Flora MacDonald, a strapping girl of noble birth from Inverness. 'Hamish was a romantic at heart,' she insisted in answer to a letter from Justice Baldwin. She may have been right. But experience rather than romance was what Hamish stood in need of, at the crisis of his life on a lonely island, eleven and a half degrees north of Capricorn.

The preparations for his first betrothal, he found, were in themselves unnerving. In Funafala the traditional bridal suite is a canoe, seven feet long and the finest wood, decorated with stained sinnet and cowie shells. The Commissioner's wedding feast was followed by a six-hour song and dance ritual known as the 'aloa meke'. This lasted well into the evening. Eventually, bedecked in flowers, Hamish McKenzie and his bride were laid ceremonially on the nuptial litter in the centre of the canoe. Mounds of sweet potato, bananas and coconuts were piled around them. 'Even lovers must eat,' cackled the matrons of honour, pushing them adrift. Along the shore the moonlight glinted on the palm fronds. 'We're painfully cramped in here,' protested the Commissioner as the narrow craft lurched out on the ebb-tide. Forty-eight hours later the islanders were out again to greet him with further dancing as he paddled ashore by the morning light, triumphant if seasick.

During the ensuing months Hamish McKenzie followed the Lunar Calendar with increasing confidence. Partner succeeded partner in the bridal canoe. It was not until the end of a year's strenuous activity that it occurred to the

Commissioner that something might be going wrong. He decided to hold a secret conference with the elders. 'Had they learned of any results?' he inquired. Their intelligence system, he knew, was foolproof. 'No,' they reported sadly, 'the first signs of the Harvest have yet to appear.' The Commissioner was disappointed. He was not, however, a man who gave up easily. 'A dogged hooker,' McKenzie's rugby master had always said of him. He decided to ignore the Lunar Calendar, thereby accelerating Schedule A. Rarely can one man have worked with such devotion to the Imperial Service. Or with so little success. Yet he would not admit defeat. He redoubled his breathing exercises and flung himself desperately into a fresh programme. Night after night, morning after morning, and even in the afternoon, Hamish McKenzie would be off, à deux, across the lagoon. By now the Scottish pine had wilted into a sapling. All without avail. Commissioner McKenzie began to walk like a man repeatedly struck by lightning.

It was in this sad state that Mr Justice Baldwin found him. And to the judge he poured out the whole story, confirming every extraordinary detail by referring to his files and to the inhabitants of the island.

The judge, tight-lipped, lost no time in pronouncing Schedule A 'and all regulations pertaining thereto — *ultra vires*'. He also ensured that the Commissioner was quickly retired. Hamish McKenzie ended his days in Bournemouth, haunted by what he considered an inexplicable failure.

It was left to Mr Justice Baldwin, in the course of a protracted enquiry, to provide an answer. As the judge noted, at page 96 of his handwritten judgement, the probable explanation for the failure of McKenzie's bizarre Schedule A was a botanical one. There grows on the island of Funafala a vine-like creeper known as *Desmodium dependens blume*. When boiled, this plant produces a juice known as *savasava*. As the judge points out, *savasava* is often reserved by the Funafalans for persons of great distinction. 'The impressive dignity of its formal presentation,' writes the judge, 'cannot fail to engender a feeling of pride in the honoured recipient.'

'*Savasava*,' he proceeds, 'also induces temporary sterility, a fact unknown to the Funafalans in those early years, but undoubtedly the reason, also, for the extraordinary degree of population control in these tiny atolls.'

From every point of view, the judgement concludes drily, Commissioner McKenzie clearly exceeded his powers.

Chapter Fifteen

A Bird in the Bush

'Good to see you again,' said JS, gripping my hand with painful enthusiasm. 'Must be over a year since you last had to call?' JS kept the peace single-handed in his remote territories with only an occasional need for a visit by me.

'Blasted nuisance this case you've come to do,' JS observed as we were landing in a very bumpy sea. 'My fault the whole thing. No need for an Assize at all but for me. Been frightfully cut up about the whole wretched business. Hadn't even the heart to ask you to robe in the usual style. Hope you don't mind?'

'Not at all,' I assured him.

I was even more relieved to see that he had changed his car since my first visit. This one was only about thirty years old, roomier, and without a dicky.

'Should never have bothered with Guy Fawkes Night,' he continued.

I was sitting in unexpected comfort alongside him.

'Guy Fawkes?' I began, 'don't quite . . . .'

'Simple enough,' he went on. 'Decided to celebrate November 5. Manufactured a lot of fireworks. Islanders joined in. Great fun. Unfortunately some young bloods from the village ran a bit out of hand. Got hold of my home-made jacky-jumpers. After a long drought, 'fraid that was it.' With a screech of brakes JS drew up alongside the charred remains of the Residency.

'Hasn't worried me of course,' he said, 'much prefer a tent.'

As he spoke the figure of Narle emerged from the rear of the canvas quarters with a broad smile of welcome. He deposited my belongings inside the guest wigwam assigned to me for the night.

'Had to report the damage to Government HQ. They

85

instructed me to charge the lads with arson,' continued JS, resuming the saga during supper. 'Damned shame really.'

Arson was an offence which could only be tried by me as visiting Assize Judge. JS would much have preferred to dispose of the affair under his powers as magistrate, but this was not possible.

Apart from the odd cane field conflagration between feuding cane farmers, arson was a rare crime in the islands. This was in some ways surprising, as the firing of villages and the smoking out of enemies had once been a traditional form of tribal warfare.

Over Narle's strangely brewed coffee, JS made one of his infrequent references to his absent spouse.

'Heaven knows what Edith would have had to say on the subject,' he exclaimed. 'Used to go into one of her nervous fits even if I smoked in bed. Was even going to raise the alarm one night when all I'd done was to drop my cheroot into her embroidery bag.'

'Where is the lady of the house — the establishment — at present?' I inquired politely.

'Still at the Spa,' said JS.

'Pardon?', I said.

'Leamington,' barked JS. 'Living with her mother. Finds the natives more friendly there.'

After my especially long journey out to the island I was hoping for an early night.

'Won't be able to lull you to sleep on the ivories, old boy,' explained JS. 'Afraid the harmonium went up in the flames.'

However, JS's other musical possession — the gramophone — had escaped the holocaust.

'Have to make do with Harry Roy and his Hot-Cha-Ma-Chacha Boys,' were my host's good-night words.

'Got some new needles, too,' he called, with a note of triumph.

The needle may have been new, but the heat of the fire had unquestionably warped 'The Sheikh of Araby' — another of JS's favourites.

Harry Roy opened his vocal at a rattling pace, but slowed into a sepulchral groan on the line 'Into — your — ter-r-nt — I'll cr-rr-ee-ee-pp.'

At this point the canvas parted and a shadowy figure appeared. With his usual sense of timing, Narle had brought me a night-cap of brandy and water.

I settled back on my camp-bed and began to light my pipe. 'No good, Sah,' whispered Narle, rolling his eyes heavenwards. Puzzled, I followed his pointing finger. A gap in the tent roof had been patched with what looked like a piece of coloured canvas. As my first puffs of smoke cleared, I found myself gazing at a portrait of an angular lady in a Lenglen bandeau. Her expression was reproachful.

'Memsahib no like fire in bed,' said Narle.

Edith may not have approved of the safari life, but JS had found a useful role for her after all. I dreamt that night I was billetted in the Sistine Chapel, but otherwise I had a sound forty winks or so.

'Rise and shine,' shouted JS from the adjoining tent. He directed me to a portable shower set up behind the flame trees.

It was only a short walk, after breakfast, to the Island Court House. This was a large thatched building where JS himself normally dispensed a kind of makeshift justice. Throngs of villagers were pouring towards it from all directions. From the merry calls which greeted me, it seemed I was recognised from my previous visit.

'You've got a better turn-out than I usually manage,' said the Commissioner, leading the way into the shady interior lined with native mats and warclubs.

One wrinkled elder seemed to show a special interest in me.

'He says he has links with your homeland,' JS translated.

'Has he been to Wales?' I asked, surprised.

'I think, rather, Wales has been to him.'

The old man nodded bright-eyed as he chattered on.

'It seems his grandfather ate a missionary from Wales. Welsh by absorption might be the best way of putting it.'

I wished him well and hastened to my seat. It was the huge upturned cooking-pot, the usual substitute in these parts for a chair. But with the old man's gaze upon me, I opted for the bench against the wall, with JS alongside me.

The court building was now packed to capacity, but as the

sides were open to the lagoon, we enjoyed a pleasant sea breeze.

It was the task of JS to announce the Proclamation which traditionally opened an English Assize, a duty he obviously relished.

'Oyez, Oyez, Oyez,' he began. 'All manner of men having anything to do before His Lordship the Justice of Assize draw nigh and give your attendance.'

At this point a large green parrot flapped in and settled between us on the Bench.

'I don't think you've met Henry,' said JS.

He dug into the pocket of his bushjacket and began to feed the visitor.

'Been a great pet of mine for the last year,' he explained. 'Little blighter follows me everywhere.'

Henry was gobbling rather offensively.

'Surely not into court,' I demurred.

'On the contrary,' said JS, 'he always sits up here with me.' He produced another handful of peanuts.

Just then the gaoler brought in the five young arsonists. They stood behind a couple of banana crates. There was a buzz of excitement at the back of the crowd.

'Court,' called JS to silence matters.

'Cawk,' said Henry.

'Better get on with the hearing,' I decided. I requested JS to put the indictment to the defendants and ask them how they pleaded. He interpreted in fluent vernacular. 'How do they plead?' I asked.

'Not Guilty,' relayed JS.

'Nark Gilkey,' echoed Henry. His black eye was severe.

'He's learned to imitate my more familiar court pronouncements,' explained JS.

'So I gather,' I observed, 'but this is a serious case!'

I pulled myself together with an effort.

'He must be taken away.'

The parrot was now scratching through my copy of the Depositions.

'It may seem very odd by our standards,' was JS's reply, 'but a parrot is venerated in these parts.'

I had to admit that the presence of the bird seemed to be

taken for granted by everybody else in court.

'Look at those old ladies over there. They're looking at him as if he was the Archbishop of Canterbury,' declared JS. This, strangely enough, was true.

For an instant my mind flashed back to the court in Arabia, where Mr Bhindi had tethered his camels. It never seemed to strike the local people as odd when my Assize was turned into a sort of menagerie.

'One of their tribal gods was the Great Green Parrot,' JS continued. 'In the eyes of the populace here, believe it or not, Henry adds dignity to the court.' He gave the feathered deity a reassuring pat on the head. 'Don't you, Henry?'

I signalled to the Court Usher.

'Could you bring my set of the *Laws of England*,' I requested. He did so and upon my instructions he stacked the volumes between myself and the parrot. 'Let the trial commence,' I declared, having at least blotted Henry out of my immediate gaze.

Apart from an occasional twitter, the bird remained thankfully silent while the case proceeded. The evidence was overwhelming. The defendants had obviously taken advantage of JS's amateurish experiments with fireworks. Mischievous intent seemed clear. The moment arrived for the verdict. I summed up the case and announced that I had found the charge proved.

'Mr Assessor,' I said to JS, following Section 18 of the Criminal Procedure Code, 'what is your opinion?'

'Not Guilty,' declared JS.

'Nark Gilkey,' agreed Henry, choosing his moment to hop up on to the top of my law books.

'That's two to one, old boy,' said JS.

'JS,' I whispered sternly, 'do you seriously think I can accept a parrot as a member of the Bench?' I was quite determined. 'He must be removed from court,' I said, 'however sacred he may be.'

'Well, I'm not taking him out,' said JS, 'and you'll never get anyone else to do it.'

I was anxious to avoid an untoward scuffle single-handed with the creature, especially if, as I feared, Henry emerged the victor. 'Then where would British Justice be?' I reflected.

An adjournment was the only solution.

'Would you kindly retire with me, Mr Commissioner,' I said. I stood up and bowed to the assembly. 'Alone,' I added, with what I hoped was a meaningful glance at the parrot.

JS and I conversed together in the small antechamber behind the main hall. Henry remained in court.

'Come, come, JS,' I said. 'You know perfectly well the correct verdict is guilty.'

JS produced a spotted bandana handkerchief and trumpeted loudly. 'True,' he said, 'but as I've already explained, I really began the whole affair. How can I let them end up in prison?'

After considerable discussion, I hit upon a compromise. 'I'll sentence the youngsters to serve their term extramurally,' I explained. 'In other words, they can work their sentence by rebuilding the Residency, and that'll be the end of the matter.'

'Done,' agreed JS.

We returned to court. From his seat on the law books Henry had kept order during our absence. The audience waited in silence. We took our seats and I turned formally to JS.

'What is your verdict, Mr Assessor?' I repeated.

'Guilty,' declared JS.

'Gilkey,' confirmed Henry.

I decreed that the defendants should do as we had agreed. The decision satisfied everybody, especially Henry. He accepted with lordly aplomb a procession of tribute from the reverent populace — mostly peanuts, with an occasional melon rind. It was, I supposed peevishly, in its ludicrous way a scene comparable with the medieval tradition of sanctity associated with English Law. 'One has to be flexible about such things,' I told myself.

As Halsbury comments: 'It is in the pomp of the Assize Court that the vigour and power of the ideal of justice is really brought home to us . . . . One gets a sense of a great engine of justice, powerful and all seeing, of checks and counter-checks which it is impossible to evade . . . .' Certainly Henry had qualified for the last clause.

Next morning JS was down at the wharf to bid me farewell. Henry was on his shoulder, still keeping an eye on things.

'Let's hope you're not planning a fireworks display in the

91

Court House next time,' I called, as my launch moved out from its mooring.

'Not Guilty,' said JS with a reassuring wave.

'Nark Gilkey,' called Henry, across the iridescent sea.

Chapter Sixteen

The Best of Both Worlds

'Between you and me, sport,' said the Australian pilot who first flew me to the Savage Isles, 'this part of the world is a bonzer little paradise.'

I was sitting with him up front, our only other passengers being a cargo of hymn-sheets for the Savage Islands Brass Band.

As he spoke the plane stalled violently. We had run into an electric storm. There was a clap of thunder and a vivid flash bounced off the right wing.

'Y'see,' he shouted, wrestling with the controls, 'that's what comes of travelling with the flaming law. Bring any digger bad luck.'

'Shall we share a hymn sheet?' I quipped, masking considerable apprehension on my part. 'What about 'Abide With Me'?'

He was too busy to answer, peering down through the mist for the landing strip. He managed to find it safely and, once down, helped me good humouredly to unstrap my trunk of law books from under the rear petrol tank.

'Maybe the Law brought you luck this time,' I said, pointing to a battery of small holes in the side of the trunk where the lightning had struck.

The peace and order of the mini-airport, trimmed with hedges of pink hibiscus, contrasted with an earlier description I had read. A smiling customs official, wearing a flower behind his ear, waved me past his bamboo desk. It was rather different for Commodore John Bryan (Foul Weather Jack), in 1832, who commented, 'The inhabitants of these parts are proverbial for their cruel and barbaric habits. From what we ourselves have witnessed, they are rightly named the Savage Islands.'

93

Some fifty years later, however, the Superintendent of Christian Missions in the South Seas was able to report, 'Our toil in these heathen lands has borne great fruit. The eating of human flesh has become extinct. Polygamy is fast dying away. Infanticide is declining. With the coming of the British Flag human life is no longer reckoned cheap. The avenger of blood comes not now as a stealthy assassin or backed by savage warriors. But invested with the solemn dignity of Established Law.'

I took my leave of the Australian pilot.

'Orrightmate!' he said, with a farewell punch in the chest. He walked back towards his plane. 'Wotch out they don't swipe yer bleeding wig-box,' he called. 'The Queen might fancy it to keep her tucker in.'

As the aircraft taxied away for take-off, a landrover drew up beside me.

'Alloa,' welcomed the driver, a dazzling young man in a mandarin-style tunic with blue and gold epaulettes. Etuate was the name by which he introduced himself. He was the nephew and secretary of Fatu Hova V, reigning Sovereign of the British Savage Islands Protectorate.

'We have to go straight to the Palace,' he explained.

I pointed out that the journey had been rugged in the extreme. I was in dire need of a barber and hadn't seen a shower bath for several days.

'I'm afraid Her Majesty is very infirm,' Etuate told me. 'On doctor's orders she can only manage an audience this afternoon, before retiring to her country retreat for a long convalescence.'

We drove at a sedate speed through the island capital of weatherboard stores, thatched houses, and corrugated iron chapels. A party of school children waved from a footpath under the flame trees. I remarked that one or two had fair hair.

'Souvenirs of the war, Aunty used to call them,' laughed Prince Etuate. There had been several hundred Allied soldiers stationed on the islands during the 1940s.

We circumnavigated the coral walls of the Palace. As we passed through the open gates Etuate turned on the wireless. 'An anticyclone lies over the Queendom,' announced the local radio. 'The weather will continue bright and clear.'

The new paint on the Pacific-Gothic turrets of the Royal Palace glistened in the sunlight. Past silent lawns we edged our way to the main verandah of the Royal Residence. At the foot of a wide flight of steps he stopped the vehicle and a palace guard — appearing from nowhere — opened the door for me.

Etuate conducted me into the Palace. It had the tranquil air of an English manse at the turn of the century. There were antimacassars and photographs of various royal personages, including King Edward VII and George V.

'Her Majesty Fatu Hova V,' announced her nephew.

The Queen, a grandmotherly lady in a Chinese dressing-gown, was propped up on a dais of finely embroidered mats. She fingered a string of blue prayer-shells. About her the walls were hung with Victorian prints of biblical scenes — gifts from the missionaries, no doubt — *The Return of the Dove to the Ark*, *Ruth in the Gleaning* and *Abraham with Isaac*.

I made my salutation in front of *The Disciples* by J. Arbuthnot, ARA, a canvas of enormous size.

I badly needed a change of clothing and a haircut, while my three-day growth of stubble was particularly disfiguring.

'An interesting likeness,' said the Queen, pointing to Mr Arbuthnot's representation of Judas Iscariot, immediately to my right. I tried to change the subject.

'A significant honour for me, Ma'am,' I began, 'to serve as your new Chief Justice.'

'It's of great importance to us too,' said the Queen. 'You're the sixth in line of succession, you know. May I ask your denomination?'

'Middle Temple,' I replied. The Queen cleared her throat.

'I was referring to your religious convictions.'

'Oh, C. of E.,' I blushed.

The Queen looked relieved.

'I thought you might be an unbeliever like so many white men these days. And that would be the one bar to your appointment.' She handed me a Royal Parchment and a pen. I clocked in under the Royal Cipher and the ceremony was over.

Outside, Etuate was waiting to take me to the Judge's Lodging, a gloomy edifice erected in 1890 with imported terracotta for the first Chief Justice's visit.

'I'm so sorry you caught my Aunt on one of her off-days,' were Etuate's final words as he left me to settle in.

For the next hour or so I worked steadily at the marble washstand in the vast uncurtained bedroom.

'Better put the rest of my clothes away,' I decided, fairly satisfied with my respectable new image in the mahogany standing mirror. The chest-of-drawers was lined with the yellowing pages of the 'Empire Stores Shopping List, Pall Mall, 1911'. My clean handkerchiefs went on to the sheet advertising 'Twilfit Rustproof Corsetry for Memsahibs Everywhere', while my pyjamas covered the descriptions of 'Wilkinsons Mixture — Pronounced by the Highest Authorities as the Most Wonderful Purifier of the Human Blood and the Safest and Most Reliable Remedy for Torpid Livers in Hot Climates', 'Huxley's Ner-Vigor Tonic for All in Imperial Service who feel Unable to Work through Enervation and Nervous Debility' and 'The Blue Nile Ointment for Severe Inflamed Conditions of the Skin, Dhobi-itch and Other Equatorial Eruptions'.

A polite knock on the bedroom door interrupted my reading.

'Arta-noon tea ready, Sah,' called a man's voice. I went out to be greeted by Samuela, the cook, a white-haired Savage Islander with several broken teeth. He had laid out tea beside a long-sleever cane chair in the dining-room.

'You do this job long time?' I inquired.

'For life, Sah,' he beamed.

I stirred the sugar into my tea.

'You must really like the work then,' I observed thoughtfully, 'to want to stay here for ever.'

Samuela looked puzzled.

'I get life, Sah,' he said.

He pointed through the open window. At the bottom of the magnolia garden a wicket gate swung open in the ocean breeze. There was a rusty board on it. 'H.M. Gaol', it read.

Samuela passed me a plate of hot buttered scones.

'Are you a prisoner then?' I asked.

He nodded. 'The only one,' he boasted.

I took a puzzled bite of the scone.

'You've certainly cooked this very nicely,' I approved. 'What was your crime?'

'I kill my daddy,' he replied. 'Give bad food. No pain. He go down dead very quick.'

I spent an uneasy post-prandial half hour until Etuate arrived with the case files for court next day.

'He's perfectly safe,' he reassured me. 'It's not a habit of his. It was his father's land he was after.'

He paused politely while my stomach rumbled.

'Let me know if you'd like a royal food-taster though. We have one we could spare.'

I laughed it off and turned to the files.

'Poisoning of livestock' met my eye.

'At least they've moved on to the animals,' I reassured myself.

Most of the cases were appeals from the courts of the native magistrates. It all seemed pretty straightforward, I thought, as I duly made my way next morning into the Second Drawing Room of the Judge's Lodging, which constituted my court-house.

Etuate called on the first case. Two local advocates, unqualified by English standards, but renowned for oratory, tiptoed into the chamber. Each squeezed into a tiny desk at opposite corners of the room.

'Why are they so cramped?' I inquired.

'Normally — in good health — the Queen herself presides over the court,' explained Etuate. 'It's taboo for the head of a commoner to be higher than hers. To make sure this doesn't happen with the advocates, they have to conduct their cases sitting in desks borrowed years ago from the infants' school!'

'An appeal under the Land Law,' began the appellant's advocate. The preamble to his case he read in the traditional manner, sitting down. 'Under the law of these islands,' he explained, 'my client, as a landlord, is bound to give every male in the village an acreage of land once he becomes of age.'

I made a careful note of all this.

'But,' he continued, 'this right involves an obligation to plant the required number of coconuts.'

At this point the portly advocate decided to take advantage of the absence of the Queen by way of a standing oration.

'The respondent,' he declaimed, 'has shamelessly neglected those obligations.'

98

Unfortunately, as he got to his feet the desk rose with him.

'I'm sure a rearrangement of the Bar would assist the course of justice in this case,' I decreed.

Proceedings were eventually resumed upon the substitution of a table for the desks.

I reversed the decision of the lower tribunal and ordered the respondent to plant the required 200 coconut trees on the land in the following season.

We moved on from the Land Case to 'Miscellaneous Appeals'.

In the last of these Prince Etuate recited the facts himself.

'Volo ordered a dugout canoe from Jaki and gave him five dollars for it. Jaki did not make the canoe because Hovolu took three dollars from him. Hovolu did this because he had supplied his father Soru with a stick of tobacco, part of which was given to Dini, Volo's father. Dini did give Soru two dollars for the tobacco and also for some turtle he had supplied. Soru still did not pay Hovolu, but spent the two dollars. Soru has now promised to borrow a dollar to give Hovolu and Hovolu has paid three dollars to Volo and promised to make him a canoe. When the canoe is finished Volo is to pay over three dollars. The native magistrate has ordered that the two dollars are to be handed over within two months and the canoe completed within three months.'

Etuate sat down behind a spray of ferns.

'Something of a tangle,' I murmured. 'Who exactly has appealed?'

'Everybody,' replied Etuate.

He bent a kindly ear in my direction. 'It may not be quite as difficult to resolve as you think,' he said. I wondered why. 'I understand,' continued Etuate, 'that none of the appellants is still alive. Rather an old case I'm afraid.'

Time, I discovered, had its own special meaning in the Savage Isles.

This brought my opening session to an end.

'There's just the criminal trial for tomorrow,' said Etuate. 'Case of shopbreaking.'

It was all that remained for me to deal with on that particular visit.

'I'll leave you to study the prosecution evidence,' he said.

Prince Etuate's command of English was not surprising,

since he had been educated abroad. But the overall high standard I had met in the island capital was due to the Mission teaching. This was where the local magistrate had been schooled. He had recorded the statements of the prosecution witnesses with copperplate precision.

The accused, it seemed, had been seen leaving the shop in the early hours of the morning, with a large carton of Coca-Cola balanced on his head and a dozen pairs of Aertex Y-fronts — two products of the West which had most impressed him. Three by-standers had intervened to deprive him of his loot, but failed in the struggle. The one flaw in the case was that none of these witnesses had been asked by the police to identify the accused on a parade.

When I joined Etuate in the Court Drawing Room, next morning, the first thing he did was to pull on the bell rope.

'A little refreshment before we swear in the jury and start the case,' he said.

I pushed an open volume of Halsbury towards him.

'I'm afraid we can't start the case at all,' I replied, waving away the tray of orange drinks. 'Your police don't seem to have heard of the law on Identification Parades!'

I read from the relevant paragraph in Volume 22.

'The defendant selects his position among eight men of similar appearance to himself and the witnesses are each given the opportunity to pick out the accused.'

Etuate handed me a glass from the salver.

'Identification of this defendant may not be the problem you imagine,' he suggested.

'Out of the question,' I snapped. 'English criminal law is littered with cases of mistaken identification — from Oscar Slater onwards. Matter of principle.'

At that moment the defendant appeared in the doorway to surrender to his bail. His face was tattooed with stripes of red and green. He wore a large boar's tusk through his nose.

'He's the hereditary high priest from the last of our heathen islands,' explained Prince Etuate. 'Fell into crime on a visit to the capital.'

'Does he always look like this?' I asked faintly.

'He's no alternative,' said Etuate. 'Goes with the job. It's all done at his initiation ceremony.'

Not unexpectedly, the jury convicted before midday.

100

I ordered the defendant to join the cook in the garden penitentiary where I paid a last visit with Etuate before leaving for the airport. The shopbreaker stood cheerfully to attention to greet us. He had a half-empty bottle of Coca-Cola in his hand and was clad simply in crisp new Aertex Y-fronts.

'The quality of mercy is not strained in these islands,' said Prince Etuate. 'The shopkeeper let him keep a couple of samples of his haul.'

'Christian charity,' I approved.

'And a heathen prayer for increased profits in return,' rejoined Etuate with a final handshake. 'It's the best of both worlds in the Savage Isles, wouldn't you agree?'

Chapter Seventeen

McKenzie in Togoland

'Hamish McKenzie,' I reminded my friend the archivist at the Royal Colonial Institute. 'Should you chance upon anything connected with his earlier career, please let me know.'

When in London I had found the Institute a useful retreat in which to carry on with this book. The Archivist, Mr Robinson, had shown a kindly interest in its progress. 'The truth about McKenzie,' I explained to Mr Robinson, 'has always been difficult to pin down, because of the many legends that circulated about him in the South Seas.'

The following December he sent a postcard to my home in Wales. 'The truth about McKenzie!' he wrote. 'Much better than fiction. Do come and see for yourself.'

Upon my next visit to London I called on him again in his dusty vaults off Trafalgar Square.

'These,' he said, 'are the papers of Sir William Hucknett, Chief Justice of Togoland, 1903 to 1912.' The papers filled four large boxes marked 'Pears Soap'.

Apparently the African Bureau had been researching the 1906 Anglo-French Conference on Togoland, over which Sir William had presided. 'Under the Agreement that followed,' explained the Archivist, 'the British were allotted the Western administrative areas of Lome and Lomeland, Misahohe, Kete-Krachi and Yendi, while the French received Anecho, Atakpame, Sokode and Sansanne Mangu.' He extracted a heavy file from Box Number 3. 'The Commissioner assigned to Lomeland was none other than your bizarre character from Funafala — Hamish McKenzie!' he exclaimed.

We carried the dossier into the Reading Room.

'You'll see that Commissioner McKenzie functioned as a

Magistrate, Class 2,' he continued. 'In that capacity he managed to leave something of an impression on Chief Justice Hucknett!'

Sir William Hucknett, it emerged, had kept a special file of all records and correspondence relating to appeals from Hamish McKenzie's Magistrates' Court.

'When you've read these,' laughed Robinson, 'you'll understand why the Colonial Office tried to lose Hamish in the vastness of the Pacific Ocean.'

He switched on a reading light and left me to it.

One point soon emerged from my studies. Typically, Hamish McKenzie had attacked his judicial studies with extraordinary zeal.

Cattle trespass was the first matter which occupied his indignant energy. Within three months of his posting to Lomeland, he had impounded almost the entire livestock population of the area. It was this news which first brought his name to the notice of Sir William Hucknett.

Not long after Sir William had managed to rectify this bout of magisterial hysteria, the Sessions Judge at Yendi was rushed home on sick leave.

'Have we a replacement?' Sir William had minuted to his deputy.

'Only Hamish McKenzie,' was the answer.

'He'll have to take over immediately,' noted the Chief Justice.

Hamish McKenzie seems to have arrived at Yendi in his usual kilt and tam-o-shanter. He was therefore obliged to borrow his predecessor's regalia for the actual court-sitting. The gown he found he could wear, but the wig was impossibly small for his great highland head.

As those familiar with the early construction of a Judge's Bench-Wig will know, strips of stout fabric are latticed into a frame on to which the horsehair is sewn.

With considerable ingenuity, Hamish's native orderly fashioned for his master a much larger frame, using slender bamboo lathes and filling in the gaps with coconut fibre.

All went smoothly during the first part of the session. Unfortunately however, as time went on, the rising humidity in the Court House affected the bamboo frame. As McKenzie himself explained in a subsequent letter to the Chief Justice, 'the under-lathes began to curl outwards'. Then, apparently, the cross-strut started to let out 'cracking noises'. At first Mr McKenzie was able to control this development with insertions of pieces of the *Togoland Gazette*. But the situation became completely out of hand when, *without warning* — the underlining is McKenzie's — 'the central latitudinal strut clamped itself firmly over his ears'. Apart from the discomfort this caused, a far graver consequence was involved. Hamish McKenzie found he could no longer hear the evidence.

It is a tribute to his fortitude, which he later displayed in other circumstances on Funafala, that McKenzie continued the hearing. Or, rather, he continued to preside over the hearing. Sadly enough, his endurance merely provided the defendants — alleged slave-traders — with a successful ground of appeal. They had not been slow to observe McKenzie's plight.

The appeal papers duly arrived on Sir William Hucknett's desk in the Togoland capital.

'Upon no account,' ruled Sir William in a brisk judgement, 'should evidence be shut out by the Panoply of the Law.'

Although for one reason or another, many of Hamish McKenzie's later decisions were reversed on appeal, he always maintained a tenacious belief in the principles of British Justice. 'Nobody is above the law,' he wrote.

Indeed, his rigid adherence to this particular maxim led to another weird document in Sir William's Pears Soap Box.

McKenzie, it appears, had returned from a trip in the bush one afternoon. He was stumping about his Commissioner's bungalow when he discovered that mosquito larvae had started to breed in stagnant water on the back terrace. This was an offence under the Togoland Hygiene Ordinance.

I pictured the Commissioner sitting up late that night battling with his inner self. Whether he did so or not, the record is clear that he made his way the very next morning to the Government Health Office. He called for the Sanitary Inspector.

'Inspector,' he announced. 'I have infringed the Mosquito Law. I order you to prosecute me.'

Before the astounded official could protest, the Commissioner seems to have carried on with his normal daily duties.

The action McKenzie had taken meant that he would have to try himself, since there was no other magistrate within 500 miles.

'I could hardly inconvenience Government in a summary matter for which I alone was responsible,' he subsequently explained.

There could have been few parts of the territory where McKenzie's fame had not already spread. It can be taken for granted that his court was unusually crowded on the morning of the trial.

The Sanitary Inspector read out the charge. McKenzie pleaded guilty. Resuming his seat on the Bench, he proceeded to deliver judgement. 'This type of offence,' he said, to the now empty dock, 'is in no way trivial. The least punishment I can properly impose is a fine of £75.'

The bemused spectators must eventually have dispersed, but it was probably some time before the Court Clerk could bring himself to speak. 'A remarkable case, sir,' was a likely remark.

There was no reply, I suspect, from Hamish McKenzie. He was giving the matter a great deal of further thought.

At last he stood up.

'A gross miscarriage of justice,' he declared — and indeed recorded. 'A fine of £75 was clearly excessive for a first offence.' There was nothing else for it, McKenzie resolved. 'Shall have to appeal against sentence to the Chief Justice,' he announced.

The overland safari to the Chief Justice's Court must have taken him days. Red-eyed and weary, he obtained an early hearing before Sir William Hucknett.

Sir William was obliged to listen with equanimity to this incongruous application. McKenzie argued his point with blinkered enthusiasm.

'No,' adjudged the weary Chief Justice, 'I can see no mitigating circumstances. The Trial Magistrate was correct in imposing a substantial fine. Appeal dismissed.'

McKenzie returned, without flinching, to his lonely station. He was disappointed. 'But at least,' he observed, in a covering Minute to Sir William, 'the due processes of law have been correctly pursued to finality.'

From my investigation of Sir William's 'McKenzie Records', I came to a conclusion. The Chief Justice, even at this stage would, I believe, have borne with McKenzie's mulish adherence to Legal Dogma. However, a final judicial episode erupted in Lomeland two years afterwards, which the Chief Justice could not overlook.

It originated through no fault of Commissioner McKenzie. He received a visit from his aunt.

Dame Fiona McKenzie was herself an unusual person. She had travelled adventurously with her late husband, McKenzie McKenzie of that Ilk. During her journey out to Hamish she became the first white woman ever to navigate the Volta River during the rainy season. It was typical of her that she had not warned her nephew of her imminent arrival. She arrived at his residence just before Sunday tiffin, at the head of a train of exhausted bearers.

'Where are you, Hamish?' she called.

The Commissioner was practising his favourite sport — tossing the caber.

'Guid God,' exclaimed Hamish, dropping the trunk in surprise. As the caber was necessarily of heavy banyan timber it was fortunate that nobody was injured.

Aunt Fiona's first engagement, she insisted, was to observe her nephew at his magisterial work. Next morning, clad in a large beaver hat, she supervised the placing of her canvas chair in the well of the court.

A young man stood in the dock charged with abduction.

It was the tribal version of the Bride of Young Lochinvar, so McKenzie subsequently recorded.

It seemed that the accused had eloped in the night hours with the daughter of the Chief of a rival tribe. The pair had been stopped in their flight by the flooding of the main river. The angry father and his supporters had recaptured the luckless couple. The bridegroom stood woebegone, awaiting the verdict of British justice. He had already undergone tribal punishment by beating.

The Magistrate was about to pass sentence when he was interrupted from below. 'Release the prisoner at once, Hamish,' ordered Aunt Fiona.

'Silence please,' said the Magistrate. But Dame Fiona, on

her feet, was already addressing the gallery.

'The young man has done nothing wrong,' she declaimed.

'Aunt Fiona, I must ask you to sit down,' intervened the Magistrate more loudly. 'Abduction cannot go unpunished by the law.'

Dame Fiona stood her ground.

'Rubbish,' she cried. 'I eloped with your Uncle, or rather he eloped with me — after a little persuasion I admit. Nobody was blamed for abduction then, and nobody is to be blamed now.'

Before the Magistrate had time to recover from the revelation, Aunt Fiona had brought out from her handbag her Chief Guide's jack-knife, a possession which accompanied her everywhere. With a firm tread she advanced towards the padlocked dock. 'Hold hard, young man,' she commanded. The defendant boggled. There was not a moment to be lost.

'Take Dame Fiona below,' the Magistrate decreed above the uproar in the court. 'She is committed for contempt.'

A prison sentence for his militant relative would present even greater problems. It was as much as the court staff could do to get her back to the bungalow. So Aunt Fiona spent the next few days under house arrest, confined to her room.

'I must emphasise, Aunt Fiona, that you are permitted to appeal against my decision,' Hamish explained, joining her for morning coffee.

'I've drawn mine up already,' she snapped, 'as well as altering my will.'

The appeal papers were rapidly forwarded to Sir William Hucknett.

'Not McKenzie again,' yawned the Chief Justice when the folder was placed before him. But his jaw remained hanging at the sight of the name of the appellant. He reached a decision in record time. 'The prisoner is to be discharged forthwith,' he decreed.

Sir William prepared an urgent dispatch to the Colonial Office in London.

'By his own lights,' he wrote, 'Commissioner McKenzie is a dedicated officer. Regrettably, however, his sense of balance has been progressively disturbed, possibly from bouts of

Togoland Fever. His posting to a more congenial climate is strenuously recommended.'

The Chief Justice suggested Pitcairn, the remote island home of the Bounty mutineers. But this was turned down. The Colonial Office feared another insurrection from the hot-headed descendants of Fletcher Christian, if Hamish McKenzie were appointed their overseer. The people of another Pacific atoll, Funafala, it was decided, would be more accommodating. In a sense, the Colonial Office proved right.

Chapter 18

The Parish

'You seem to have had a judicial parish of millions of square miles,' said Mr Robinson.

I was again at work in the Reading Room of the Royal Colonial Institute and we had been discussing the geography of the second part of my book. He was turning the globe which stood in the large bay-window. As it creaked to a standstill, the retired Chief Botanist of New Guinea clicked his tongue disapprovingly. A shower of dried leaves of the deadly Vai-vai swamp plant fell to his feet from the specimen album he was examining. Three of four elderly memsahibs, at work on biographies of their late husbands turned from their researches at the India table. 'Was the notice for silence totally ignored these days?' one of them demanded.

'From San Sebastian in the Shebas,' I whispered, 'up here to Rambau, and westwards as far as the Savage Isles.'

He peered at the large blue segment of Oceania spanned by my hand.

'Your parishioners were largely fish, then,' he jested. 'Including plenty of sharks, no doubt?' He stifled a wheezing laugh in his handkerchief as we stole out behind the memsahibs.

We made our way down to the sub-basement, a vast cellar of early colonial history. Perching myself on a Victorian fire-extinguisher, I explained to Robinson that the only sharks that had ever caused me problems had been human ones. A Brazilian property developer for instance. He was snapping up islands for sale to film stars.

'Had to protect the islanders from that kind of exploitation,' I said.

'And he wasn't the first,' my friend replied. 'Sharks like that had been around the South Seas as far back as the sixteenth century. They were after gold.'

He waved his hand round the shelves.

'It's all recorded in here,' he said, leaving me to my researches.

And it was.

The mysterious source of the Queen of Sheba's treasure was thought to be in the South Pacific. The sixteenth century Spanish Navy had no doubt about it and their Commander named what became my western judicial boundary, the Sheba Isles.

'Possession,' noted a Spanish chronicler of the time, 'was taken in the name of His Holiness the Pope and the King of Spain. And having rested a little, the Commander appointed officials, both royal and municipal . . . . the Superintendent of Mines, the Magistrate of the City and the Magistrate of the Gentry.' The gentry, however, as I read on, proved to be 'hostile devils with poisoned arrows . . . . and there was neither city nor mines, only rude huts and deadly fevers.'

I turned to another shelf. *The Pacific Order in Council of 1875* hardly sounded an exhilarating title. But the jurisdiction exercised through it by commanders of visiting warships produced some remarkable stories.

In 1883, for instance, Commander FitzWilliam D'Arth had occasion to try a slave-trader captured off San Sebastian. Leading Seaman Pickles was the main prosecution witness. He had been injured in the gun battle with the slaver.

'Hold up your right hand, Pickles,' ordered Commander D'Arth, about to record his testimony in the form of a Deposition.

'Can't, Sir,' said Pickles. His right arm had been broken in the fracas.

'Hold up your left one, then,' said the Commander. Pickles cleared his throat.

'Sorry, Sir,' he explained. 'That one's gone too — bit of grape-shot.'

'Well hold up your leg, man,' FitzWilliam D'Arth had replied. 'You've got to hold up something if you're going to be sworn in a court of law.'

I found myself wishing I'd come across FitzWilliam before. I could have effected this decree on a number of occasions with useful effect.

Naval commanders were duly replaced in the course of

112

years by judicial commissioners. By the time I arrived there, cases were varying from murder to marine insurance, whaling to war damage, compulsory purchase to carnal knowledge.

Appeals were of less variety but of greater difficulty in the neighbouring territory of Sabusabu. My earliest predecessor in the South Seas, Sir Charles St. Stephen, had ended his days there as President of the Court of Appeal. He had drafted the Ordinance under which the Appeal Court functioned. It was Sir Charles's obsession with English legal tradition which accounted for the title still afforded me as President of the Court, namely 'Master of the Rolls'.

Sabusabu comprised three islands, each of which had a resident local judge. Two of these judges sat with me, to constitute the Appellate Court, to hear appeals against a decision of the third. Rivalry between each of them was intense. My extremely arduous task was always the same. It was to dissuade whichever judicial couple happened to be with me not *automatically* to reverse the decision of their absent colleague!

I moved on 300 miles south-east of the Shebas to another shelf. The New Orkneys had also been within my appellate jurisdiction. The Spanish had been there, as well, in the sixteenth century but Spanish influence had long disappeared, save for a judicial ghost. Jointly administered since 1905 by Britain and France, the New Orkneys had a British resident judge and a French resident judge. There was supposed to be a third judge appointed by the King of Spain.

I searched in vain through the records but it seemed he had never materialised. I like to think of a spectral arbitrator hovering over the Bench in Spanish ruffles and ringlets whenever the British and French judges disagreed.

A distant banging interrupted my researches. It was strange how deep in these caverns of imperial archives, noises in the building mingled weirdly with pictures from the past. The boom of the first floor dining-room gong seemed to echo the wardrums of the Papuan head-hunters. The creaks and rumbles of the lift shaft just above my head reached a crescendo as I came to the story of the ambush by warriors of Captain Shields, RA in the Bazuto jungle. It was also curious that the sound of hymn-singing from the Methodist Assembly in the adjoining building drifted in just as I reached a vivid description of the conversion by the missionaries of the crocodile-worshippers of Lake Nyesa.

Something drew me to the upper shelves. It wasn't an easy ascent. Each step up the book ladder provoked a minor landslide. *Among Boers and Basutos* by Mrs Berkly caught me a sharp crack on the temple as I missed my footing on *Our Travels in Poona and the Deccan* by Arthur Crawford, CMG. This started an avalanche from the Polynesian section. J. Nettleton's *A Grim Story* (*Transactions of the Melanesian Society*), followed swiftly by *South Sea Rambles and Scrambles* by Sundowner, (Major O.B. Shanks of the Poi-Poi Volunteers), culminating in six volumes of the *Oceanic Languages* (their Vocabulary, Grammar and Origins) by Humphreys and Schofield, (Auckland Theological Press).

On the topmost pinnacle I eventually arrived at a particularly familiar landmark, *Rambau — Its History and Development*. A picture fell out from the book. It was an etching of the British landing by an eighteenth century ship's artist — sailors under the palm trees exchanging tobacco for breadfruit with native girls. It all looked rather different from my first view of the island. By that time phosphate had been discovered and the excavators had been at work for sixty years. I circled a grey lunarscape of the worked-out rocks in a Pan-American Dakota.

'How does it grab you,' asked the navigator as we peered down at the ghostly peaks and valleys, 'being Chief Justice of the Moon?'

The community into which I landed lived on the fringes of what was left of the island. They now had considerable revenue from phosphate royalties to compensate them for the loss of their homeland, so their little wooden houses were scattered around with what looked like brand-new fridges and motor-bikes.

'As soon as they go wrong they buy another one,' explained the Police Chief, an Englishman, who greeted me.

I turned to inspect the guard of honour of Rambauan policemen — six stalwart figures in tropical khaki and sunglasses.

'The pick of the Force?' I murmured.

'This is the Force,' he answered with a trace of irritation.

My surprise was unnecessary. The people of Rambau were law-abiding, although the case I had to try that day was memorable. The defendant was charged with attempted pigslaughter, to me, at least, a novelty in my criminal calendar. In the failing light of dusk he had run down a kerb-crawling sow, whom he claimed to have mistaken for his wife. There was a history of domestic friction.

'Just wanted to teach her a lesson,' he explained.

Fortunately it was a bicycle he had been riding and the pig was now happily adjusting to its leg splints, her date with the oven temporarily postponed.

A voice from below summoned me back to the present. Mr Robinson had returned and held out an illustrated Victorian publication.

'Pitcairn,' he said. 'Thought you might be interested. Ever go there?'

I had indeed, and we sat down to talk about it on an island of stacked encyclopaedias.

'Always been fascinated by these first impressions of Fletcher Christian and the *Bounty* Mutineers,' said Robinson, 'when after searching nearly 10,000 miles they found a home.' He opened the book.

'The island,' he read, 'exceeded our most sanguine hopes in its fertility, its beauty, its temperate climate. We found coconut trees, yams, breadfruit, taro, sweet potatoes, appai fruit and abundant water.'

'I actually met Fletcher's great-great-grandson, John,' I interjected. 'He was Chief Magistrate of Pitcairn, a wiry little chap, in European clothes, half-English looking, half-Tahitian.'

'Did he have any relics of his famous ancestor?' Mr Robinson wanted to know.

'Yes, his Bible,' I told him. 'They used it at the school. He had one of Fletcher's waistcoats, too, rather tattered but much prized.'

At that moment a summons ⸱om a visitor took the archivist away. I turned the pages. What a quaint place it had been. I remembered John Christian's unique way of talking, English faltering into pidgin, but with the West Country intonation of his eighteenth-century ancestors.

'Any particular problems on the island?' I had asked him.

'Not enough men,' he laughed. His slanting black eyes twinkled.

'We live strictly,' he assured me. 'There was one boy from Pitcairn, a jolly makin' sort of feller. Went to New Zealand. Came back with new ideas about us men sharin' ourselves out with the womenfolk. I goin' to hev to put an ole goatskin on you and send you jumpin' from rock to rock with your brothers!'

The book on Pitcairn set out 'The Laws of 1839'. Like the Tablets of Moses there were ten of them.

Law No. 1 provided that 'The Magistrate is to see all fines levied, and all public works executed, and everyone must treat him with respect'. There was a law for Dogs, a Law for Cats, and a Law for Hogs. Law No. 9 was headed 'Trading with Ships' and stipulated that 'no females are allowed to go on board a foreign vessel . . . . without the permission of the Magistrate; and in case the Magistrate does not go on board himself, he is to appoint four men to look after the females'. The final law, No. 10, read, 'Any person taking the public anvil and public sledge hammer from the blacksmith's shop is to take it back after he has done with it; and in case the anvil and sledge hammer should get lost by his neglecting to take it back, he is to get another anvil and sledge hammer'.

The ten Laws hardly suggested an island riddled with serious crime. Yet, of the nine mutineers who had settled on the island in 1790 — Fletcher Christian, Midshipman Edward Young, Botanist William Brown, Assistant Gunner John Mills, John Adams, and four other seamen from the *Bounty* — all but two were murdered.

Ill feelings had developed between the six Polynesian men, who had arrived with the mutineers, and the Englishmen. Each of the latter had brought to Pitcairn a Polynesian wife. In 1792 the wife of seaman John Williams died. Williams replaced her with the wife of one of the Polynesians. So began the jealousies which led in 1794 to the murder by the Polynesians of Fletcher Christian and four other Englishmen. On the other side, four of the Polynesians were killed. By 1800 John Adams was the sole survivor of the mutineers. Until his death, thirty years later, Adams exercised a firm patriarchal rule. Pitcairn was free of serious crime from his day onwards.

'Our prison,' as John Christian told me, 'is just big enough for two. But they don't often get that far.'

'Well, you're the law here now,' I said to John Christian. 'Would you have taken it into your own hands like Fletcher did?'

He rubbed his deeply tanned face thoughtfully. 'When I visited England,' he said, 'I saw the ship of Nelson at Portsmouth. I saw the whips they used in those days. You know what? I don't blame Fletcher at all. He was in the right.' He shook his head and grinned. 'If it 'ad bin me, I'd a' done more than turn Bligh loose in a long boat, I kin tell you.'

For whatever reason, John Christian's ancestor had chosen to give his captain at least a remote chance of survival. One of the reasons for that remarkable survival was another island called Waika. Bligh had obtained food and water there which helped him on his dreadful voyage to Timor.

Before leaving the Colonial Institute that day I had time for a last chat with Robinson. I told him I had a story to contribute to his archives about a subsequent visit by Europeans to Waika, so far unrecorded by historians. I had come across it because Waika was another island in my parish.

The visit in question was that of Lady Frampton and her second husband in 1869. It was Lady Frampton's first visit. Regrettably, as we shall see, it was also her last.

Chapter Nineteen

Prohibition in the Cannibal Isles

Among celebrated lady travellers — Isabella Bird, Lady Hester Stanhope, Miss Gordon Cummings, Marianne North, Lady Jane Digby — the name of Lady Bertha Frampton has been overlooked. This is strange. Certainly in the case of Lady Bertha, she, along with Darwin, Lincoln, Gladstone and Poe, was one of the most remarkable people born in 1809.

At the age of sixty, Lady Frampton surprised Walter, her second husband, by taking him out to the Cannibal Isles. Had he not played the harmonium at her temperance meetings in Boston, Lincolnshire, this would not have happened, for it was there that they met. Walter suffered from chronic acidity and could not digest fermented drinks.

'I have had the call for some years, Walter,' she announced three weeks after their marriage. Lady Frampton had visited the South Seas four years before upon her way back from Melbourne with her late spouse, Sir Horace Frampton the evangelist. 'Horace and I saw more alcoholism in those islands than amongst the working classes of Boston,' she explained to Walter. The Frampton's ship had called at Lovaka, the then capital of the islands, where, as my predecessor Sir Charles St. Stephen discovered, liquor was cheap and plentiful.

'I sent Horace ashore with a bundle of tracts,' Bertha recalled. 'The poor man's health was never the same again.'

Fortunately, Sir Horace had left his widow comfortably endowed.

'I'm a very lucky man,' Walter assured himself. He was not quite so sure of this when she booked their passage to the South Seas. However, they had the steamer's best accommodation, from which Walter would emerge to view the blue waters of the Pacific. Then he would perch all day, like a sparrow, at the foot of Bertha's giant chaise-longue on the sun-deck.

'Bertha cannot abide intemperance,' he explained in conversation with the Chief Officer, 'particularly among the cannibals.'

The Chief Officer nodded approvingly. Lady Frampton, voluminous in her silks, reminded him of his days under sail.

The voyage lasted several months. At last on 16 May 1869 they reached Lovaka, the capital of the islands.

They stayed with Edgar Bayard, the British Consul. He was an old friend of Sir Horace Frampton. They retired early to the guest room at the Consulate which adjoined Lovaka's principal hotel, the tin-roofed Polynesia. The noise from the bar grew more riotous by the hour.

'Now can you hear for yourself how sorely they need temperance here?' cried Lady Frampton, throwing back the mosquito net. Walter, his little pink ears flattened between the pillows, smiled wistfully. 'Poor ignorant natives,' she sighed, 'poisoning their systems with alcohol.'

Lady Frampton was not to know that the natives were excluded from the hotel. The islanders had other ways of poisoning their systems. On 21 April 1865 for instance, they had cooked the Reverend Joseph Barker, Wesleyan Minister of Wagagadelevitu, in his wellingtons, and downed him, boots and all.

'The worst alcoholism is in the outer islands,' lied their host, at breakfast next morning. 'Why not start your temperance work out there — say at Waika?' He could think of no island in the group more distant from Lovaka and after a weekend of barley water, Her Britannic Majesty's Consul was desperate.

Three weeks later Lady Frampton and Walter arrived on the American brig *Charles Doggett* at the island of Waika. Lady Frampton, bone-corseted in the prow, supervised the unloading of Walter's harmonium into the long boat. The Chief of Waika, forewarned of their visit, awaited them on the shore. Lady Frampton viewed him through her opera glasses. 'A slovenly, nasty looking fellow,' she commented. What the Chief of Waika though of Lady Frampton is not recorded, but he had learned from the fate of his cousin that it was wise to affect hospitality towards white visitors.

His cousin, Chief Waradadua, chief of the neighbouring village, had believed himself invulnerable to gun-shot. A blackbirding party from the *Stanley*, a Queensland slaving ship, found the Chief unwilling to trade his people for calico and washing blue. Fighting broke out, during which the Chief strutted defiantly in an exposed place. A rifle shot killed him before he could fully appreciate his mistake. His death was, however, revenged by the people of Waika who ambushed the slave-dealers on Waika beach. Their captain and two companions took refuge on a high rock. At dusk the captain decided to go down to negotiate a truce. He was promptly seized and suffocated head downwards in the water, cooked and then eaten. His shattered comrades managed to escape during the night.

'I wish to make it quite clear,' Lady Frampton announced to the Waika Chief as he helped her on to the white sand, 'that I have not come here to be eaten.'

The Chief looked hurt.

'And as for my husband,' she added witheringly, 'you can see for yourself what a poor dish he would make.' Walter was paddling ashore, his striped trousers rolled above his knees.

'I intend to open a Cocoa and Reading Room on the island,' she explained to the Chief, later on, through an astounded interpreter. 'My mission here is to wean you away from the foul intoxicants to which I know you are at present addicted.'

Next morning the Chief of Waika arranged for a formal presentation of yagona to the visitors. Yagona is made from the dried root of a shrub. It is mixed in a large four-legged wooden bowl. The tanoa, a wooden bowl, is placed at some distance from the Chief, with its plaited cord and white cowrie shells laid out towards him. When the yagona is ready, the cord is wound up, the cup-bearer moves forward, his cup filled. Then he turns to face the Chief. Holding the cup with his arms fully extended, he lowers his body until his knees are fully bent, every muscle taut, and fills the Chief's cup. The Chief drains the cup, and amid hand-clapping and cries of 'thah' (empty) he spins it to the mat.

When Lady Frampton was presented with the yagona she

assumed that it was alcoholic and instantly threw it away. Apart from the fact that it was not, of course, alcoholic, her action was an unforgivable insult. The Chief said nothing at the time.

It happened that a site had been prepared in the village for the erection that day of a new bure (house) for the Chief. The house was to be 78 feet long, 36 feet wide and 10 feet high. Its centre post, already hewn to shape and polished, was four feet in circumference. The woven bamboo for the walls and the reeds for the thatched roof had been collected. Before construction could begin, however, a living person has to be buried upright, clasping the great central post for the ridge pole. Such a sacrifice was believed essential to strengthen the mana, or mystical power, of the Chief.

'Our little white man,' observed the Chief, 'is obviously too insignificant for such an honour.' He glanced approvingly at Lady Frampton's massive biceps. 'Place her in the pit,' he directed.

Out of feelings of delicacy, the islanders conducted Walter to a house on the opposite side of the village while the ceremony was carried out. Faintly he heard the traditional chant 'The lowering of the post' — the words of which were still known when I was in the South Pacific.

During the next few days the new widower sat quietly by the lagoon watching the breakers curl on the reef. 'I like it here,' he decided. Fortunately the Chief had taken a liking to him. In those days it was fashionable among the leading island Chiefs to boast a tame white man amongst their entourage. Walter was permitted to stay on the island for the rest of his life. He was allowed two 'wives', whom he selected with meticulous care.

According to the Waikians, Lady Frampton, once having passed over, acknowledged her mistake. She approved of yagona-drinking. So much so that the yagona ceremonies held in the new bure, over which her indomitable spirit presided, were always occasions of good omen, until the Waika Chief took to whisky-drinking in his old age. A particularly drunken orgy on Christmas Eve 1896 seems to have proved the final straw. 'Quite enough,' Lady Frampton decided, and let go the centre post. The post crashed down, killing the Chief and two of his companions.

However legendary this last part of the saga, Lady Frampton's influence definitely lived on in the Liquor Prohibition Laws which I was required to enforce. Consumption of alcohol on the islands was strictly controlled by a permit system.

The Waikian elders, from whom I heard the story of Lady Frampton, agreed to take me to the site of the chiefly bure. It lay on the edge of the main village. The thatch had collapsed and the site was a mass of creeper.

'The centre post is still where it fell,' I was told. 'It has never been moved.'

I was keen to see underneath. If there was any truth in the final episode, I should find there a pile of bones and the shattered fragments of a whisky bottle.

Unfortunately the fallen post was piled high with sacred stones.

'May I dig around a bit?' I asked.

'Very sorry,' explained the interpreter, 'there is a strict taboo on the shrine. Nobody is allowed to approach within three arms' length.'

Chapter Twenty

The Rehabilitation of Young Offenders

'Temperance,' said JS, peering into his empty glass, 'never caught on amongst my family.' This, I recalled, had been apparent from the rubicund features in the portraits displayed along the top of JS's harmonium.

The Commissioner had come to stay with me in the island capital, to help in a new project of mine. He knew all about the Lady Frampton saga. 'Can't vouch for the details though,' he warned.

Our discussion of the sad end of the intrepid Lady Frampton was interrupted by a commotion on the upper verandah of my house.

'It's the housekeeper,' I explained. 'We're having your bed moved out of your bedroom.'

JS bounded to the foot of the stairs. 'Just shove it against the wall,' he called.

The housekeeper hurried down to refill his glass.

'Much more important,' approved JS. He tilted his right elbow towards the ceiling. 'The only homestead among my relatives where you couldn't get a drink was Cousin Dot's,' he said. JS always held his tumbler from above and funnelled down the alcohol. 'Mind you,' he went on, 'it wasn't temperance with Cousin Dot. Just meanness.' He took a healthy bite of watermelon from my fruit bowl. 'When Cousin Dot died,' said JS, 'we found a large sack amidst her belongings. It was labelled 'PIECES OF STRING — TOO SHORT TO BE OF ANY USE'.'

After washing down several pounds of kashew nuts with his drinks, JS settled back under the fan.

'Now tell me all about this Youth Club idea of yours,' he said.

It was in order to get the club going that I had invited him over.

'Youngsters drifting into the capital away from traditional village disciplines — unemployment — getting into trouble with the law — increase in juvenile delinquency,' I outlined the problems. 'I've persuaded the Roman Catholic Mission to let me have the use of the Church Hall for these lads,' I explained. 'Trouble is, I haven't had much response so far from the young people themselves.'

JS stirred the swizzle-stick in his tumbler.

'That's where you come in,' I said.

'Leave it to me,' JS replied.

He was as good as his word. 'Look in on us,' he said, two weeks later.

I was committed that day to what promised to be a lengthy perjury trial.

'Last minute snag,' announced the Prosecutor when the proceedings opened. 'An adjournment is requested for two hours.' The defendant had developed a bout of frenzy.

'He'll have to be examined by the doctor,' agreed Defence Counsel, 'to see if he's fit to stand trial.'

I retired into the Robing Room so that the doctor could be summoned.

'Good opportunity to visit the Youth Club,' I decided.

Down at the Mission Hall I came upon tremendous activity. JS was responsible for it all. Boxing was going on in one crowded corner. There was table tennis in another. A bevy of muscular youths was practising weight-lifting at the far end of the building. JS was outside conducting a First Aid Class.

Unfortunately my arrival caused a painful lull in proceedings.

'You see my problem,' I confided to JS. 'When many of these lads last saw me, they were in the dock and I was handing out their sentences from the Bench.'

JS was busily shaping a heap of palm fronds into bandages.

'How can I ever hope to gain their confidence?' I asked him.

He put away his pen-knife.

'Very easy,' he answered. 'Just fall from that acacia tree and break your leg.'

I sighed. JS could be exasperatingly frivolous at times.

126

'Only pretend to break your leg,' JS said. 'I want you to be the patient for the group to practise their First Aid on.'

I looked doubtful.

'Participation,' urged JS. 'That's the secret of success with any Youth Club.'

I began to grasp the way his mind was moving.

'It's vital in your case,' he said. 'Let them see you joining in. That way they'll begin to accept that the law has a human side.'

'JS is right,' I thought.

'Just shin up a few feet then fall back,' he said. 'Make it as vivid as possible.'

I was not prepared to go that far.

'I'll just spreadeagle myself at the foot of the tree,' I agreed.

A buzz of excitement greeted this unexpected exhibition on my part.

'Our first job, lads,' said JS, outlining the object of the exercise to his team, 'is to locate the injury suffered by the Judge.'

He bent down over me.

'You're supposed to have broken your leg below the right knee,' he hissed.

I made a show of pain in that direction.

'To find the fracture, boys,' JS continued, 'we have to compare the injured limb with its sound neighbour.'

Suddenly, and quite without permission, JS sliced off both my trouser legs with his penknife.

'It's sheer vandalism, JS,' I complained. What especially irritated me was that they were my best pair of black-striped trousers. 'I'm going to look foolish returning to conduct a serious criminal trial like this,' I said. It might not have been so bad had JS cut the legs less jaggedly, or at least to an equal length.

'Nobody will notice anything's wrong under your gown,' said JS. 'And you'll feel a great deal cooler in court.'

The First Aid Class of delinquents was now helpless with laughter. It took JS a few minutes to restore order.

'Let's assume the break is here,' he said. Using a dampened guava stick he tattooed a cross under my knee cap. 'Next we look around for splints.'

One of the class ran down to the shore and returned with a pair of canoe paddles.

'A bit on the large side,' said JS, 'but they're certainly strong enough.' Under his supervision, one paddle was placed under me and the other on top.

'Pull on the injured leg below the fracture,' instructed JS, 'then bind fast the splints.'

There was no shortage of volunteers for this operation.

'For goodness sake JS,' I protested, 'tell them they're not supposed to be weight-lifting now.' I suppose the youths themselves were not conscious of their strength.

'How does that feel?' JS inquired.

It was not so much the weight of the splints that concerned me as their disproportionate size.

'I'm very boxed in,' I said. It was almost as though I was in a three-quarter-length coffin.

'Place your left forearm across the chest,' said JS, 'with the palm towards the body and thumb upwards.'

'What good is that going to do?' I wondered.

He placed my elbow in the middle of a broad coconut frond.

'We're assuming you've also broken your collar bone,' JS explained.

I remained gloomily silent while eager brown hands encircled my upper body with a tight girdle of pampas grass.

'Final exercise,' announced JS, 'Stretcher-Bearing!'

It transpired that the First Aid Class had already made a litter for this purpose, using branches of rain-tree bound with sinnet.

'Lift the patient on to the stretcher,' JS directed. Shielding his eyes from the sun, he pointed to the headland which rose steeply behind the Mission compound. The Cable and Wireless Station lay on the top.

'For the purpose of this exercise,' said JS, 'the Cable and Wireless Station is our nearest Medical Post.'

A narrow path led through the bush behind the Catholic Mission and followed the contours of the headland up to the Telecommunications Building.

'We'll have a bit of a competition,' said JS. 'One relay team will carry the Judge up the path. The other will bring him back.'

128

He called on the first two runners.

'Josefa and Samueli,' said JS by way of introduction. 'Athletic fellers, both of 'em.'

I knew both candidates well. They had recently been paroled, after a period of detention given by me for causing grievous bodily harm.

'Keep the litter steady,' said JS as we set off.

My carriers negotiated the first stage of the journey well enough.

'Speed it up,' called JS from below. He was timing us with a stop-watch.

The next two members of the Outward Team were poised at the take-over mark. This was at a point where the track turned sharply above the northern slope.

'Don't forget the Judge has to be back in court very soon,' yelled JS, 'in order to punish his current batch of evil-doers!' This was perhaps true, although I would not myself have mentioned it at that particular moment.

'O.K., Boss,' grinned Samueli. He said something in Waikian to Josefa and they broke into a sprint towards the take-over junction.

I am almost sure that what followed was due to over-keenness on their part. I did feel that Josefa was rather showing off when he disengaged his right hand in order to snatch a yellow thornflower and place it jauntily behind his ear. But I have no evidence at all that they were deliberately not taking proper care of me.

As we swerved into the bend I could, of course, feel that I was at an angle. And I rather think I called out a warning, 'Remember lads, I've nothing to hold on to,' just before the final catastrophe. Certainly I might have been better prepared for it had my view of things not been hopelessly restricted by my foliage of bandaging.

From the excited voices of the waiting pair of runners there is little doubt as to the ultimate cause of disaster — they tried to pass me over without the slightest reduction in speed. Whether or not somebody stumbled so that the stretcher completely overturned 'on the snatch', as it were, I cannot say. What I do recall is the plunge down the bank into a bush of wild lime. Then, I'm afraid, I blacked out.

'Sorry about that, old boy,' JS's familiar boom was the first sound I heard when I recovered consciousness. I opened my eyes to find him peering down at me. 'We've sent for the doctor,' he said.

I was back in the Mission Hall, propped up against the ping-pong table.

'The doctor's delayed at court,' said JS. 'Apparently he was needed there to examine a prisoner.' He looked sympathetic.

'Yes,' I said, 'I know all about that.'

I could feel that I was badly bruised. What caused me greater concern, however, was the growing conviction that my judicial career was somehow the subject of some doom-laden conspiracy. All designed to place me in embarrassing predicaments, some of them almost farcical.

My embittered reverie was interrupted by the arrival of the doctor.

'Ah, here you are, Judge,' he began. 'I've been waiting to give you my report on the defendant in the perjury trial.'

He finished tapping on my ribs and turned me on to my side.

'The defendant is fit for the trial to continue,' said the doctor. He paused, his hand pressed tellingly on my collarbone. 'Which is more, I'm afraid, than I can say for you.'

JS collected me from the Outpatients' Department next day.

'Well you don't need my help any more,' he declared. 'So I'll be off back to my station.' He handed me a walking stick. 'As far as the Youth Club's concerned,' he said, 'from now on, you'll never look back.'

I tried to look pleased.

'You gave them a chance to practise *real* First Aid,' said JS. 'They'll never forget it.' He helped me into the taxi.

'Neither will I,' I replied. Not for the first time I could think of nothing more original to say.

Chapter Twenty-One

Miss Wotherspoon's Island

Miss Wotherspoon's Island is easily missed. Tasman never found it, Bligh avoided it, Cook, blown off course by a hurricane, nearly ran into it. I managed to land there safely in a local copra boat.

'Where will I find her?' I asked the skipper. I had arrived to take evidence on commission from Miss Wotherspoon, an invalid spinster too frail to travel to the court on the main island in the Western Oceanic Group.

'She lives on the plantation,' he answered. He pointed to a patch of green beyond the beach. 'Think you're wasting your time, though,' he added. 'Sounds rather like a lot of red tape this Government Inquiry of yours.' He had agreed to pick me up later, on the evening tide.

'I haven't come all this way for nothing,' I assured him.

He shook his head. 'It's a weird place in any case,' he said. 'And as for Miss Wotherspoon. . . !'

With the sun glinting on the pink coral, against a dazzling backcloth of hibiscus and oleander, the island looked enchanting.

'Wait until it gets dark,' warned the captain. 'None of the workers on her plantation will go out except in daylight.'

I made some wry comment about superstitions of Polynesia. He shook his head.

'It's an island of ghosts,' he insisted.

I threw my briefcase on to the jetty and sprang ashore.

'Well, Miss Wotherspoon doesn't seem to mind them,' I laughed.

She was, I knew, the only European on the tiny island, which she had inherited a few years ago from her father, Major Wotherspoon. The Major was a descendant of early English settlers from the mainland.

'It's different for her,' called the copra-master, returning to the wheel, 'she's . . . .' The rest of his words were lost in the wind as he swung his craft out to sea.

A few minutes brisk walking through the coconut groves brought me to a clearing. A tropical garden to the left of the main drive seemed to be ornamented with large boulders.

'A pygmy Stonehenge?' I wondered. I had always been a keen amateur archaeologist. I pulled aside the creepers on the nearest stone. There seemed to be traces of ancient hieroglyphics carved into the surface.

With some excitement I put on my spectacles and read 'Called to Higher Service, Algernon Wotherspoon June 29th 1903'. I had merely stumbled on the family cemetry.

There were no less than a dozen similar monuments, and the last of these was freshly decorated in the traditional native style with streamers of coloured grass. From here I looked up and saw the house ahead of me. It was a great rambling bungalow crammed with the flotsam of 100 years of squirearchal living, South Pacific style.

'Anybody at home?' I called, taking a few more steps. The main room was full of Victorian chairs and tables squeezed up next to a huge Hawaian day-bed. Landseer prints on the walls rubbed shoulders with native axes and ceremonial whales' teeth.

'Blue, tending to mauve,' said a voice from the shadows.

'Ah,' I jumped.

A very pale lady in a barkcloth shawl was examining me from a wicker chair on the opposite side of the parlour.

'Miss Wotherspoon, I presume?'

She put down her lorgnette.

'I'm Judge Overton. No doubt you received my letter. Have to take testimony on commission from you. Hope that's convenient?'

'More mauve than blue,' repeated Miss Wotherspoon.

'Sorry?'

'Your astral body, young man,' she said.

She pulled up a cane table with a walking-stick and rang a bell. 'At least you're in time for tea,' she continued.

I sat on the edge of a sofa.

'As you know, Ma'am,' I plunged on, 'from my letter that is. Government has sent me to inquire into the appropriate

royalties payable for crayfish trawled in this area of Oceania.
I've been asked to take evidence from you on customary
fishing practice in the islands. Government feels your
knowledge will be especially useful in the Inquiry.'

Miss Wotherspoon continued to gaze through me, as it
were. 'Distinctly mauve,' she muttered.

I glanced over my shoulder. Apart from a little dandruff
on my collar, I could detect nothing.

'I thought the astral body only appeared after one was
dead, Miss Wotherspoon,' I japed.

'It all depends,' she replied quietly. 'Sugar or lemon?'

A native girl had glided silently in with a silver tray of
Dresden china and, equally silently, out again.

'Lemon,' I said.

My hostess poured a delicate cupful of tea from a fluted
urn and handed me a silver dish of sliced lemon and a guava
sandwich.

'On second thoughts, I think I'll take sugar,' I said.

'A vacillator,' reproved Miss Wotherspoon. 'Mauve always
goes with vacillating characters. My late father was quite the
opposite. His astral body is bright red, of course.'

'Is he still around then?' I asked. It seemed as well to
humour the old girl.

'He most certainly is,' was the reply.

'I noticed some decorations on the last grave,' I said. She
nodded.

'It's the anniversary of father's death tomorrow.'

I swallowed the rest of my sandwich rather too quickly and
unlocked my briefcase. 'What I have to do, Miss Wotherspoon,' I said, 'is to record a few pages of evidence from you.
It won't take long.' I opened my Court Notebook.

'There's a comfortable bed for you in the guest suite,' she
interjected, 'but you may be a little troubled by the bats.' She
pointed to a vast *ivi*-tree which overshadowed the East wing
of the house. Dusk was falling and from its branches I could
hear the shrieks of its webbed inhabitants.

'I shan't be staying overnight,' I said, 'but it's kind of you
to offer.'

The noiseless servant girl removed the tea things and lit
the kerosene lights. 'Thank you, Tupou,' said her mistress.
The whites of Tupou's eyes rolled in my direction as she

withdrew. The only sound, apart from the bats, was the hissing of the lamps.

'Must be very lonely for you out here,' I remarked.

Miss Wotherspoon pointed through the shutters to the long deserted sweep of grey sand curving into the distance.

'Dreadfully overcrowded,' she replied.

I ventured a discreet laugh.

'With spirits,' said Miss Wotherspoon.

I unscrewed my fountain-pen firmly. 'If you would just answer a few questions about crayfish,' I began.

'All the Departed Souls of Polynesia gather here,' continued Miss Wotherspoon, 'on their way to Nirvana.'

'A sort of refuelling station,' I murmured. The joke fell flat.

'It's the last shore they touch before the long sea journey to the Great Beyond in the far West. But for some reason father doesn't seem to want to take the plunge with the rest of them.'

I tried a no-nonsense approach.

'All I need to know,' I said briskly, 'is what fish have been traditionally caught in this and neighbouring islands. Now I understand that as a child you used to go out with the local fishermen?'

Miss Wotherspoon cocked her head to one side.

'It's him,' she said. The shutters were rattling a little — no doubt the breeze was blowing in from the sea.

'Was it customary, Miss Wotherspoon,' I persisted, 'for the islanders to take crayfish?'

'It's father,' said Miss Wotherspoon. 'He always seems to be especially out of sorts round about his anniversary. I wish I knew why.'

I removed my spectacles with a sigh of exasperation. 'The point at issue in the case, Miss Wotherspoon,' I explained patiently, 'is that if the islanders merely fished for tuna, then the royalties payable for crayfish will be very modest. This is where you can help me.'

There was a curious rattling sound on the corrugated iron roof overhead.

'He really is irritable tonight,' said Miss Wotherspoon. 'He wouldn't be on the roof unless he was wound up about something.'

I began to pack up my papers.

'I did hope you could help me in this inquiry, Ma'am,' I expostulated, 'but of course there's no legal obligation on your part.' While I was speaking the door opened and a bowl of dried leaves rustled in the breeze.

'Can't you possibly try and tell me what's the matter?' demanded Miss Wotherspoon.

'It's just simply that I don't seem to be getting any co-operation from you in this matter,' I replied stiffly, 'so I might as well be on my way.'

'Why didn't you tell me before?' exclaimed Miss Wotherspoon.

'I thought you realised that was the purpose of my visit,' I answered.

'I'm not speaking to you, Mr Overton,' she said, her gaze fixed upon her empty hand. 'My father has this moment come in and handed me this astral note. It reads,' she continued in unflurried tones, ' "Buried wrong way round. Kindly reverse as soon as possible".'

'So they go in for telegrams in the after-life?!' I chided.

'You should be the last person to jest about this, Judge Overton,' rejoined Miss Wotherspoon, 'when it's your presence here that has enabled him to achieve this final breakthrough.'

'Mine?' I demurred.

'You're the first white man to visit us since father's death, and you've no doubt provided that special missing link in the psychic chain.'

She took me by the hand.

'Mauve astrals often have the power.'

She inspected me with some concern.

'I notice you've turned a bit paler blue. Do you feel tired?' she inquired. 'Loss of ectoplasm is quite a debilitating experience.'

'I do feel a bit on the groggy side,' I said. 'So if you'll forgive me I'll get back to my bunk on board.' I was thinking of the medicinal brandy I had tucked away there.

'You could help with the spade work tomorrow morning,' suggested Miss Wotherspoon.

I had tried my hand in various strange ways during my time in the Pacific, but this was a case for drawing the line.

'Better left to the undertaker,' I said.

'All we have in the way of an undertaker on this island,' Miss Wotherspoon rejoined, 'is Tupou's uncle. And he put father back to front in the first place, poor man.'

'Well, I'm sure he'll get it right tomorrow morning,' I soothed. 'And that should see the Major safely off the premises.'

'Let's hope so,' rejoined Miss Wotherspoon, 'Call again next year and see.'

She rang the bell. 'Here's Tupou with the lamp to see you down the drive.'

The girl with the rolling eyes was at my elbow as I made my farewell.

The moment came for Tupou and me to pass the decorated grave. The coloured garlands shone in the light.

'Everybody make present for the Major,' explained Tupou, holding the lamp over the grave. 'Now you must put something.'

'I don't happen to have a wreath with me,' I snorted.

'Any little thing,' she hissed, 'or you get Bad Luck.' She looked pointedly at my briefcase.

'There's nothing in here,' I said, irritably snapping it open. Her eye fell on the pink ribbon around my Crayfish Inquiry File.

'Look nice,' she commanded.

The next moment, several feet of Government red tape were being plaited by Tupou into a makeshift garland.

Tupou left me at the compound gate. As I wended my way through a dark thicket of fern, I looked back and caught a last glimpse of my offering hanging lop-sided in the place of honour on top of the stone.

With a hoarse cry a large bird flapped unexpectedly across my path. 'Lucky I'm not superstitious,' I told myself.

Once on the empty shore I had a distinct feeling of something or someone behind. Perhaps it was a family of crabs scuttling for shelter when I passed. 'Extraordinary how credulous some people get,' I thought.

I arrived at the jetty to the welcoming beacon of the copra boat.

'How did you get on?' asked the skipper as I stepped aboard.

I looked back to the lights of Miss Wotherspoon's bungalow twinkling in the distance.

'You were quite right,' I said. 'It was just a matter of Government red tape after all.'

Chapter Twenty-Two

The Weight of the Law

'No offence, old chap,' said JS greeting me aboard the *Sunderland* flying-boat in Vatua bay, 'but you're the last person they should have sent on this particular assignment.' Our pilot had just brought me down into the lagoon and JS had come out in his launch to take me ashore.

Tribal rivalry had erupted on Vatua, the westernmost island of JS's archipelago and I had been ferried there by courtesy of the Royal New Zealand Air Force to hold an urgent inquiry.

'The last occasion they sent a judge to Vatua was back in Justice Baldwin's time,' continued JS. 'He was ready-made for the job.'

'Was he indeed?' I replied, piqued.

It had been an arduous trip. Disturbing though my earlier encounters with JS had been, he had never before been unwelcoming.

'I rather hope I can hold a judicial inquiry as well as my predecessor,' I said.

'Don't doubt it,' said JS. 'The point is that Baldwin — going by photographs — was at least twice your size.'

JS stooped down and helped to free me. I seemed to have parcelled myself up rather too securely with the extra length of seat-belt.

'You must be the skinniest judge in the world,' he reflected.

'Steady on,' I said, 'the weight of judicial authority isn't measured in crude physical terms.'

JS continued to stroke his beaky nose in gloomy contemplation.

'Obviously nobody's told you anything about the Vatuan people,' he said.

139

This was true. The idea had been that I should bring a wholly fresh judicial mind to the island's problems. I had been given no preliminary briefing.

'Authority is measured in size here,' explained JS. 'Size, weight and strength. It's as simple as that. Unfortunately you fail in all three departments.'

I pulled down my wigbox from the luggage rack. 'There's no pleasing you, JS,' I complained. I began to shake out my judge's gown, after tying on my collar bands.

JS picked up an inflatable life-jacket. 'Could you perhaps wear this under your gown,' he suggested.

'But it's only fifty yards to the beach, JS,' I said. I peered through the aircraft window at the glassy blue sea. 'Still, if you think one shouldn't take the risk,' I continued.

'No, no, dear boy,' interjected JS. 'I merely thought it might help to fill you out a bit.'

I was beginning to jib at JS's lunacies, especially as his remarks had now focused the attention of the pilot and the other members of the crew on to me, just as I was trying to get into my gown. A sudden gust of wind through the open hatch had somehow got the sleeves entangled with the overhead breathing apparatus.

'Dracula lives,' sniggered one of the crew, from the cockpit door.

'The Phantom of the Lagoon,' rejoined his assistant. They guffawed together in their rough Antipodean way.

I snapped myself free and turned to JS. 'The sooner we get ashore, the better,' I said.

'I'll take you straight to the Rest House,' said JS. 'We'll have a serious pow-wow once we're there.'

The Rest House, a ramshackle bungalow overlooking the bay had been stocked with provisions for my stay. JS joined me for a sundowner on the verandah.

'There's what all the trouble's about.' He pointed to a sandy atoll lying 200 yards beyond the reef.

'Vatua Bay,' he continued, 'is famous for underwater volcanic activity. About twice a century it throws up an atoll like that one.' JS helped himself to another large glass of whisky.

'That's when Vatua needs a visit from the High Court, d'y'see, to decide title to one of the new bits of land that

141

suddenly appears.' He drained his glass. 'As I say, the last occasion was as far back as Judge Baldwin's time.'

A cool breeze had sprung up. JS draped himself in a tattered hide shawl.

'Always the same trouble with a whisky bottle,' he complained, shaking out the last drop, 'too much for one, not enough for two.' Since he'd consumed nearly all of it himself, I said nothing.

'Why do the Vatuan tribes squabble so fiercely over one atoll?' I asked.

'Turtles, old boy,' said JS. He settled back with a cheroot. 'Turtles are the wariest of all creatures in these waters,' he expounded. 'When they sun themselves on the reef they know that the rising tide will keep them secure from enemies. When they do the same thing on the new atoll, thinking it's the reef, they are left stranded.' He flapped his mosquito boots in a vivid demonstration of helpless flippers. 'That's when the blighters are caught by the islanders. In hundreds. Very precious they are too. And the fighting starts as to who they actually belong to.'

JS got up and started rummaging amongst the stores for a fresh supply of liquor.

'Do they always beat their drums so loudly?' I inquired. The Rest House was at least a mile from the nearest village but the noise of the wooden drums was considerable.

'Quite frankly,' declared JS returning with some brandy, 'the rival factions here are working themselves up into a frenzy over the business.' He poured himself a tumbler of brandy. This time I asked for a half myself.

'Where do you suggest I hold the Inquiry?' I asked.

'That's the danger,' said JS. 'You'll have to hold it out of doors. No building on Vatua will hold the crowds. Hope they don't get out of hand with you. Could be nasty.'

I took a quick sip at my drink.

'Of course they'd never have gone for Baldwin,' said JS. 'Built like an oak tree d'y'see. Just what the islanders respect.'

We shared a simple meal of tinned bully-beef.

'On a diet or something?' asked JS, as I toyed with my food.

'Just digestive problems,' I replied. 'Try to keep off rich

142

foods.'

'Well you could at least try an extra yam with your meals,' he went on, 'nothing rich about that.' I nodded. In a moment he reappeared from the kitchen with a vegetable the size of a rugby ball.

'Just one of these a day could do wonders,' he said.

'What *is* all this business about building the physique, this constant emphasis on size, over here?' I demanded irritably. I was tired of slurs and determined to thrash the thing out.

'The tradition among the people,' explained JS, 'is that they're descended from a race of giants. I can show you a row of eight-foot-high stones that they say represent their early ancestors. They do their best to live up to them today — massive intakes of food, ancient body-building techniques and so on.' He bunched his shoulders playfully.

'So the news is, Sunny Jim, on Vatua, BIG IS BEAUTIFUL.' JS prided himself on his unconvincing American gangster imitations.

Once I'd seen JS off the premises I decided to get down to some legal research.

'Whatever Baldwin might have had over me in size,' I resolved, 'I'll try to make up for in the old brain work.'

There was in any event no hope of a peaceful night's sleep. The drumming seemed to be getting even louder, but I blotted it out with a few solid hours mugging up over books and papers.

I must have fallen asleep over them for I woke to find my head pillowed between Halsbury's Volume VI on Damages and Volume XII on Torts. Despite a bit of a hangover I was dressed and ready for action when JS arrived next morning.

'Have had to postpone the hearing,' he called from the path.

I suppose I had been too tensed up for the ordeal ahead to notice that torrential rain was falling.

'Can't do anything until the weather improves.' He tethered his horse to the verandah rail and hurried inside.

'Why on earth have you got all these books in your bed?' he demanded. I hastily dismantled my nocturnal library.

'Working on the legal side of the problem,' I said. JS marched through into the kitchen and flung off his hide wrap. He had an armful of under-ripe mangoes which he

143

began to munch with relish.

'Did you feel that earth tremor in the night?' he asked as I joined him at the breakfast table, where he was dipping his mangoes into a mixture of curry powder and vinegar. I explained that I had been too preoccupied to notice anything of that sort.

'Nothing to worry about,' he reassured me. 'We do get them from time to time. Now to work.' He produced a pencil stub from behind one hairy ear and began to sketch on the whitewashed wall beside us.

'Had an idea!' he announced. He drew a large rectangle. 'This is the clearing in the principal village where you'll be holding court,' he began. He etched in the surrounding bures. 'There are two tall coconut trees — here,' he marked a cross at the top of his rectangle, 'and here.' He made another cross.

'Now if I get a sort of bamboo platform slung very high between these two trees,' he proceeded, 'would you mind adjudicating from up there?' He began to sketch out a rough design.

'A really lofty perch could be very impressive,' he enthused. 'And what's more — safe! Far above the madding crowd and so on.' He turned enthusiastically towards me. I shrank slightly. There were moments when I really felt that mentally JS was almost a borderline case. One could only humour him at such times.

'An interesting arrangement,' I said. 'Only thing, I couldn't hear anything — what with the wind and so on.'

JS split open a coconut and drank from it thoughtfully. 'As you please,' he said. 'Personally I rather like the idea of crow's nest justice!'

'I think it's rather straining the adaptability of the legal system,' I continued firmly. 'As for the madding crowd, I hope I can rely on your control of the situation there.'

I pulled back the curtain of sailcloth from the kitchen window and peered out. The rain was still pelting down. JS got up to leave.

'I'll be back when the weather clears,' he announced. He looked down gloomily at my bowl of BranLax and surrounding circle of vitamin pills, all part of my regular travel-pack. 'We can only hope for the best,' he said.

144

It continued to rain throughout that day. I pursued my studies in the kitchen but to little effect. The English law of real property, so far as I could see, had little to say about Melanesian atolls. It was a gap I was about to fill, I trusted.

'Overton on the Law Relating to Volcanic Eruptions'. I rolled the title in my mind. It was an exciting thought. I was dreaming about it that night, in fact, when I was suddenly turned out of my charpoy by a very noticeable earthquake. 'The finger of destiny,' I reflected, climbing back again. 'My treatise must certainly cover Subterranean Tremors,' I thought ruefully. However there were no other shocks and dog-tired I fell asleep once more.

The morning was bright and clear. All seemed peaceful in the village with not a drumbeat to be heard. I ventured out on to the shore. The scent of jasmine, pandanus and frangipanni mingled delightfully with the salt of the sea. The waves of the reef stretched unbroken across the horizon. But where was the controversial atoll?

'Seem to have lost my sense of direction,' I murmured. 'Could have sworn that was where JS pointed it out.' I swivelled around. Looked left. Looked right. Then it began to dawn on me.

'Goodness me,' I exclaimed at last, 'it's disappeared.'

There was no doubt about it. 'Must have been the earthquake in the night! And now it had disintegrated back into the depths again!'

I was still adjusting myself to this extraordinary example of the unwritten laws of the natural world when I saw JS galloping up towards me. Before he could dismount I was greeting him with the news.

'Last night's quake,' I called out. 'It's put paid to your atoll.' He waved his hunting horn in my direction and dismounted.

'Can't hear you,' he said. I repeated the information.

'It's no good,' he said, shaking his head like a large dog. 'Got this blasted humming in my ears. My mother told me it was the cello. She took it up during pregnancy, d'you see?'

'The earthquake,' I bellowed.

'Yes, that's what brings it on,' he agreed. 'Always does.'

JS heard me at last.

'The atoll,' I shouted, 'it's gone!'

'Bless my soul,' he said. 'So it has.' He began to laugh. 'At least it didn't take you with it.' He clapped a hand on my shoulder. I was only too pleased to share his merriment. Together, we made doubly sure that the atoll had gone for good, and JS set off to transmit a radio message to the Royal New Zealand Air Force Station in Samoa.

'They'll send over a Sunderland to pick you up tomorrow evening,' he reported later in the day. 'After all, not much point in your hanging on here. Looks as if your case has been settled out of court. Divine intervention you might call it.'

We took a stroll through the feathery pampas grass. The fruit bats peered down with interest from their upside-down perches in the banyan trees. I began almost to regret having to leave such an unspoilt haven of tropical flora and fauna.

'Seems a pity I have to slip away so quickly.' I said.

'Not exactly slipping away,' rejoined JS. 'There's a tribal farewell in your honour tomorrow afternoon.'

'A friendly one, I trust,' I said. 'After all I've hardly put on much muscle in twenty-four hours.'

'Ah,' said JS, 'but the people now associate you with the Great Earth Quake. It's the biggest they've known and your arrival is obviously the reason for it in their eyes. Given you a kind of new status. Magical rather than physical, of course.'

Now that I was no longer required to sit in judgement I rather looked forward to my meeting with the people . . . .

The following day a half-circle of warriors, huge men in tarpa and warpaint, awaited our arrival on the sandy slope leading into the principal village.

In front of them was a large pit filled with stones. Closer to, I could see they'd been heated by burning charcoal to a sizzling temperature.

'Cooking ovens?' I suggested.

'Curtain raiser actually,' said JS. 'You'll see.'

'We sit here,' directed JS, indicating a flowered canopy at the summit. Around us the solemn tribesmen chanted their approval.

'Take your wig off,' whispered JS. 'They want to make you an offering.' Their emissaries discharged a pungent bowl of sacred oil over my head. 'Shows you've earned tremendous respect,' said JS.

146

'I'd never have guessed,' I quipped gamely, mopping the surplus out of my ears.

'And now the fire-walk,' said JS, indicating the smoking pit.

I looked down anxiously at my buckled shoes. 'It's not what they were designed for, JS,' I fenced.

'No, no,' chuckled JS. 'This is their show. The young braves have to walk across to prove their manhood to you.'

Green leaves had been thrown across the stones. Over the fiercely hissing arena a troupe of brawny youths romped to and fro with shouts of triumph.

The performance over, the twenty-four athletes lined up and marched towards me.

'They want you to examine their feet,' JS explained.

'Chiropody's not exactly my line,' I cringed.

'Just to confirm there's no sign of burning. Protection by the Tribal Spirits and all that,' said JS.

'We'll take that as read. Formal evidence not required,' I ruled.

At a signal from the Chief, the young men dispersed. Formal speeches followed, and the presentation of breadfruit, rolled in ritual fashion across the green.

A vividly painted gentleman was pointed out to me by JS as the island's medical practitioner. His stethoscope of shark's teeth jangled from his neck as he bent to present me with a ceremonial fan of black and white cock's feathers. He seized the opportunity to whisper something in my ear.

'Wants to know if nature's calling,' JS translated.

It was a welcome suggestion. Together JS and I made our way to where a small building covered with cowrie shells and painted barkcloth had been specially erected for the occasion. I peered inside. It was a rather special closet designed to accommodate both of us. The entire construction was embowered in dried seaweed.

'Yours is the one with the Union Jack,' said JS.

On our return, they were preparing for the dancing. The gentlemen of the band were flourishing their nose pipes.

'Here come the girls,' said JS as a scrummage of enormous ladies, with hibiscus in their hair, descended on me. I had a premonition that each muscular arm would make four of mine.

'You'd better get rid of your Western ideas of beauty,' laughed JS.

The dance itself was a sort of rock and roll cum samba. I was picked up by the leader like some sort of mascot. Soon it took on the nightmarish quality of an Amazonian excuse-me.

It seems as though all my dance-floor encounters overseas were doomed. I remembered Mrs Hak, the dwarf of Sheikh Suliman, at her husband's night-club in Arabia. But at least, then, no risk of injury had been involved.

JS seemed totally unaware of my ordeal. 'You're obviously a big hit with the ladies,' he called as I whirled past, like an odd sock caught up in a washing machine.

Never before have I been more pleased to hear the drone of an aircraft. The R.N.Z.A.F. *Sunderland* had landed on the lagoon, and the dance was abandoned as everyone crowded out to meet it. I found myself pushed along to the fore.

'Here he is,' called JS to the New Zealand Air Force officer awaiting me in a dinghy as I hobbled towards the water's edge. 'The Maker of Earthquakes.'

'He certainly looks as if he's been in a few,' said the aviator, a more sympathetic specimen than his colleagues on the outward flight.

'It's not the earthquakes,' I explained. 'It's the Trojan women.'

'Bit of a new experience for a Judge, eh?' said the officer.

'Oh, I don't know,' I said, as we roared off, 'there was a chap called Breveton in the Middle Ages.'

'Who was he then?'

I reached for my set of Halsbury, bundled safely aboard by JS. 'If you're really interested,' I said, turning up the reference, 'it was recorded in this early repòrt of 1333.'

I began to read out the extract.

'Hugo de Breveton was Edward the Third's Justiciary at the January Azzize in the Wrekin.' Apparently he had dealt out some heavy sentences on the menfolk of the region and the wives took revenge on him.

'Hys Eminence,' reported the Chronicler, 'was fulle sore wracked by ye feerce and mightie Jezebels.'

The flying-boat straightened out as we set off for home.

'And how are you feeling now?' asked the kindly New Zealand aviator.

'Sore wracked,' I said, reaching into my travel-pack for Dr Grimshaw's Medicinal Spirits.

Chapter Twenty-Three

The Skeleton in the Cupboard

'You'd better get up to a hill station for local leave,' advised the Medical Officer. Further loss of weight, even since my visit to Vatua a couple of years before, had driven me to consult him, and I was finding the coastal humidity of the island capital more taxing that season than usual. 'Get some fresh air into your lungs,' he added, 'and try to eat some decent meals.'

Icy rain was thundering down on the tin roof of the Attabhoi Guest House as I paid off my taxi-driver and checked in. The Attabhoi, a modest hostelry with decaying shutters, suited my purse rather better than the fashionable hotel on the other side of the mountain.

'It's certainly bracing up here,' I enthused to the decrepit bearer who shuffled me into my little windswept bower at the end of the north-east verandah. The poor fellow's teeth were chattering too much to allow him to reply.

It was still raining heavily when I joined Mr Attabhoi, mine host, at the festive board.

'How long do these storms usually last?' I inquired.

'Maybe three, maybe four weeks,' he replied.

Mr Attabhoi was a retired schoolmaster. I gathered from his heavy breathing during mastication that he practised yoga. The menu was strictly vegetarian.

'Feed the soul,' said Mr Attabhoi, spearing a curried bean with his fork, 'the flesh, it is to be despised.' The mosquitoes that night thought otherwise. They kept up a constant attack upon me while I was trying to work upon some reserved judgments. Eventually my lamp ran out of kerosene so I retreated to bed under the mosquito net.

'Do you have any insecticide in the house?' I asked Mr Attabhoi at breakfast next morning. Removing my plimsoll

I indicated a constellation of mosquito bites upon the instep. Mr Attabhoi fixed me with his mad burning eyes. 'I am never permitting the slaughter of life,' he decreed. This became very apparent. Indeed the scuttling of the cockroaches in my chamber that evening gave me another sleepless night. At dawn I surveyed my waxen features in the cracked mirror of Mr Attabhoi's Gothic bathroom.

'Hang the expense,' I resolved, 'might as well live it up at the hotel.' As a measure of economy I decided to get there by the local bus. Mr Attabhoi packed me a curry bean sandwich with a resigned air and directed me to the terminal.

'Thunder an Lightning Transport Service', read the giant mauve letters across the windscreen of the omnibus. 'Proprietor', continued the inscription, 'J. Ram (deceased)'. The last word was in sepia. It had been added, I assumed, by the young man who sat on the ancient bonnet chewing a stick of sugar cane. This was the loyal son of the late Mr Ram.

'All aboard,' he shouted, springing unexpectedly at the controls. There were no doors or windows in the vehicle. Clouds of dust from the mountain track swirled in as we hurtled alongside the ravine. At one point a Parsee gentleman in black coat and white leggings leapt aboard. Blinded by the dust of the interior he seated himself, short-sightedly, upon my lap.

'Afraid this seat's taken,' I called down his ear.

It was something of a relief to find myself, some minutes later, deposited with my set of law books and case files outside the hotel.

After the Attabhoi, the luxury of the place seemed exhilarating. There was even a swimming pool.

'Why not take a dip,' I thought. 'Give me an appetite for lunch.'

The hotel was full of army officers on a climbing expedition. Great tanned fellows, I gave them a sociable 'good morning' as I emerged from the bathing hut. 'Some people have the decency to keep their skeletons in the cupboard,' observed one of them waggishly over his beer.

My days in the tropics had by no means made me into a strong swimmer, but my breast-cum-side stroke does now get me along, albeit in a diagonal direction. Too late, I realized why my fellow guests had not joined me in a dip. At that time of the year the altitude made the temperature of the water uncomfortably low. By the time cramp drove me out of the pool it was already apparent that I was developing some new sort of respiratory infection.

'The last straw,' said the Medical Officer, when I reported back to him. He totted up the list of my various tropical complaints and sent me back to Britain for my year's leave.